Public Affairs Management for Business

A must-have for anyone seeking to turn institutional dialogue into a strategic business advantage, this book offers the first comprehensive managerial framework for public affairs.

Many companies need to engage in dialogue with government, but done haphazardly, this can end in failure. Other books on public affairs management focus on regulatory frameworks, policy advocacy, and public relations, while the managerial side of lobbying remains overlooked and underdeveloped. This book demonstrates that success requires a clear strategy and serves as a managerial toolbox for effective lobbying to navigate institutional relationships and drive influence effectively. It focuses on the five fundamental processes – analytical, operational, digital, strategic, and organizational – that can be tailored based on specific needs. Through theory, techniques, and practical examples, readers are equipped to immediately implement these tools in their own professional environments.

This book is suitable for all managers and consultants who need to engage with government entities, as a tool for self-directed professional development, and for students in MBA and other postgraduate business courses.

Giulio Di Giacomo serves as a Public Affairs Senior Manager at FiberCop (a KKR company), and he has worked as a public affairs manager for over 20 years in multinational companies. He has written three widely adopted books on the topic and has taught lobbying at top Italian universities for over ten years.

Public Affairs Management for Business

Managerial Tools for Successful Lobbying

Giulio Di Giacomo

Routledge
Taylor & Francis Group

NEW YORK AND LONDON

Designed cover image: Radachynskyi / Getty Images®

First published 2026
by Routledge
605 Third Avenue, New York, NY 10158

and by Routledge
4 Park Square, Milton Park, Abingdon, Oxon, OX14 4RN

*Routledge is an imprint of the Taylor & Francis Group, an informa
business*

© 2026 Giulio Di Giacomo

For Product Safety Concerns and Information please contact our
EU representative GPSR@taylorandfrancis.com. Taylor & Francis
Verlag GmbH, Kaufingerstraße 24, 80331 München, Germany.

Trademark notice: Product or corporate names may be
trademarks or registered trademarks, and are used only for
identification and explanation without intent to infringe.

ISBN: 978-1-041-08979-7 (hbk)
ISBN: 978-1-041-08978-0 (pbk)
ISBN: 978-1-003-64782-9 (ebk)

DOI: 10.4324/9781003647829

Typeset in Sabon
by SPi Technologies India Pvt Ltd (Straive)

Contents

Introduction

Every day, we see new ways in which institutions and businesses engage with one another – sometimes on highly technical issues, other times with media attention that turns these interactions into public spectacles. Yet, beyond the headlines, there's a clear wind of change blowing through the halls of power. The old-style lobbyists are being asked to operate in a brand-new arena, where institutional relations blend with communication, intersect with the digital world, and now must also grapple with a powerful new force: artificial intelligence.

The classic image of a lobbyist quietly meeting with a politician to influence decisions is quickly fading. In its place, we now find analysis, structured dialogue, policy proposals, and complex networks of real and virtual engagement. The world of institutional–corporate collaboration is changing fast, at a pace that challenges even experienced professionals. Demand is increasing, and while many highly skilled professionals are stepping in, so too are amateurs. Social media has opened up access to anyone with a message, while also creating space for misinformation, bias, and confusion. The result is a chaotic but dynamic environment that clearly requires new rules and tools.

Companies now realize that they need to engage public institutions in a transparent and strategic way. Even when companies rely on excellent consultants, they still need to rethink their internal processes. That's why the figure of the institutional relations leader should have a permanent seat at the executive table. This person must guide collaboration with institutions, manage relational risks, and choose the right tools to reach the organization's goals. We'll refer to this role simply as Public Affairs Manager, using the term in its broadest sense.

Despite the growing importance of Public Affairs, there's still no shared technical framework or structured literature to support it. This lack of clarity creates several problems. It fosters suspicion in society, creates confusion around job requirements, and forces professionals to invent their own tools, sometimes with limited effectiveness.

DOI: 10.4324/9781003647829-1

It's important to stress that *Public Affairs Management* is not the same as *lobbying*. *Public Affairs Management* refers to the structured and strategic coordination of all activities aimed at managing a company's or organization's relationships with public institutions and stakeholders. It integrates multiple tools and approaches – including lobbying, advocacy, digital engagement, and institutional communication – within a coherent governance framework. Lobbying is one of the many tools available to a Public Affairs professional, just like advocacy or social media campaigns. What's been missing is a full managerial model that explains how to organize and lead this work across different contexts.

This book offers that model. It introduces practical tools and methods that professionals can apply right away. It presents a comprehensive governance approach covering strategy, daily operations, internal organization, and digital engagement. Most importantly, it helps organizations make sure their Public Affairs function is aligned with corporate priorities, can measure results, and delivers value.

In doing so, the book creates a true "Public Affairs Toolkit," a practical guide for professionals who engage with public institutions, as well as for university and postgraduate students seeking to understand this fast-evolving field. Making these tools visible is also an act of transparency: it helps legitimize the discipline and strengthen the profession.

Just like other management disciplines, these tools can be applied in any country or organization. While the main focus is corporate, the approach is equally useful for associations and even public institutions that act like private players. As with marketing, the principles are general; they can be adapted locally as needed.

This book also serves as a self-assessment tool: a way for companies to reflect on whether they are using their Public Affairs resources to their full potential. The tools are modular, allowing for quick consultation based on specific needs. Still, the book recommends applying the full model to truly unlock the function's value.

A key theme throughout is artificial intelligence, a fast-moving, game-changing force that is already shaping Public Affairs practice. The book examines AI's role in each area of the model, showing how it can be used effectively, for example, in stakeholder mapping, sentiment analysis, and predictive policy modeling.

This work is the result of more than 20 years in the field, holding every major role in Public Affairs within multinational companies. It also reflects over a decade of academic work and collaboration with top universities and business schools. It's a synthesis of theory and practice, designed to help professionals lead the future of Public Affairs with competence, clarity, and purpose.

Chapter 1

Public Affairs Fundamentals

1.1 Lobbying, Advocacy, and Public Affairs

Let's start by introducing the main definitions of the key operational areas that make up the discipline, which we will explore in the following chapters. Let's begin with the concept of Lobbying:

- **Lobbying**[1]: a term used in the United States of America, and later adopted elsewhere, to define those groups of people who, without belonging to a legislative body and without government positions, seek to exert their influence on those who have the power of political decision-making in order to obtain the enactment of regulatory measures in their own favor or that of their clients, regarding specific problems or interests: the lobbies of professional orders, the oil lobby.

Let's now introduce the definition of Advocacy:

- **Advocacy**[2]: a civil process by which a person or a group of people seek to support a policy, whether it be social, economic, legislative, etc., and influence the allocation of human and monetary resources related to it. Thanks to the use of social media, the internet, and surveys, advocacy can guide public opinion and, consequently, direct public policies.

Advocacy exerts an indirect influence on institutions by leveraging authoritative or representative positions, as well as public opinion, whereas **lobbying** involves direct engagement by the company with political figures to shape decision-making. Notably, Advocacy incorporates the web and social media, explicitly recognizing these technologies as tools to shape public opinion. In contrast, lobbying lacks a specific reference to digital platforms, likely because it still relies primarily on traditional methods.

DOI: 10.4324/9781003647829-2

A further distinction within advocacy should technically be made between activities carried out by actors such as associations, experts, and intermediaries in general (see Section 2.2 for a specific analysis of the role of intermediaries), and actions undertaken by individuals who convey demands or requests to institutions that align with those of a company implementing an initiative in which they may be directly involved. In this latter case, we refer to **Grassroots Lobbying**.

Throughout the text, we will refer to the broader concept of Advocacy, which therefore includes the actions of all categories of actors that can be mobilized.

Figure 1.1 compares the typical targets of lobbying and advocacy initiatives. In particular, the type of advocacy defined as **Grassroots Lobbying**, by engaging third parties (beneficiaries) affected by the company's actions, can effectively amplify the company's voice with institutions. It is also worth noting that in some jurisdictions, such as the United States, Grassroots Lobbying has a specific legal and tax significance. In these cases, it is subject to dedicated reporting requirements and may be treated differently from direct lobbying for regulatory and fiscal purposes.

Now, we define Public Affairs:

- **Public Affairs**: this term refers to the strategic activities aimed at influencing public decisions and policies through dialogue with institutions, stakeholders, and public opinion. It includes lobbying, advocacy, institutional relations, and analysis of the political and regulatory landscape,

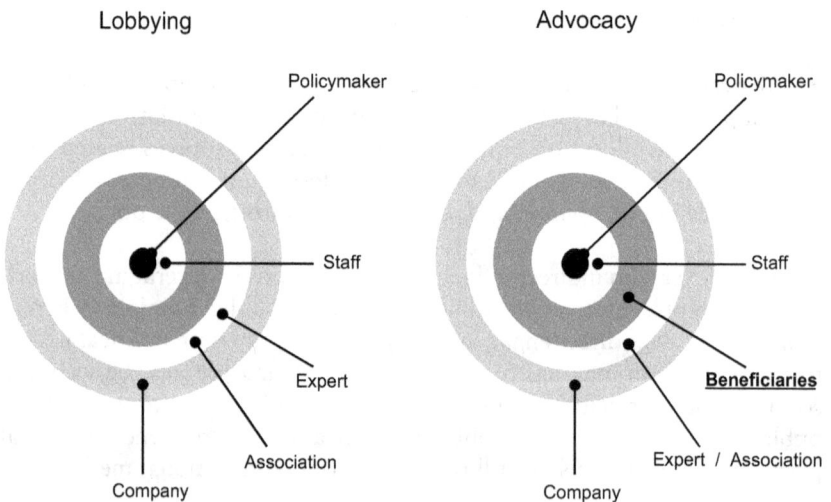

Figure 1.1 Lobbying and advocacy.

with the goal of promoting an organization's interests in a transparent and compliant manner.

When we talk about Public Affairs (hereinafter referred to as PA), we are referring to the overarching concept that encompasses all activities, tools, and stakeholders involved in both direct and indirect institutional relations between interest groups and public entities.

The last definition we provide is that of Digital Public Affairs:

- **Digital Public Affairs**: the management of institutional relations carried out primarily using digital tools, conducted from a systemic perspective, involving all actors related to a specific issue. We will see that the moment of greatest expression of "digital lobbying" occurs in advocacy projects.

1.2   The Five Basic Processes of Public Affairs

The primary focus of PA is the management of relationships between individuals and, consequently, between organizations, specifically between businesses and institutions. The ultimate objective of PA activities is to foster favorable conditions for business growth and investment enhancement.

Every interaction should always be part of a process and represent a step toward achieving a business objective. In practice, there must be a close correlation between institutional relationships and the processes for achieving corporate goals.

Let's define two categories of PA processes that respond to:

- **Explicit Relational Needs**: this refers to situations where a business or technical function must engage with a public entity on a non-procedural matter, in order to achieve a clearly defined objective.
- **Unexpressed Relational Needs**: in this context, PA plays a crucial role by accrediting the company with institutions and preparing the ground for effective message delivery.

These two categories mutually reinforce each other, and in reality, it is often observed that an initiative designed to meet one of these needs also contributes to satisfying the other. Figure 1.2 presents the five basic PA processes grouped according to the introduced categories: *Relationship Development* serves as the central process and represents the synthesis of activities since it is both the logical continuation of *Establishing Relationships* and the natural reflection of *Enhancing Investments* and *Fostering Business Development*. The *Relational Risk Management Process* aims to safeguard the solidity of the relationship over time.

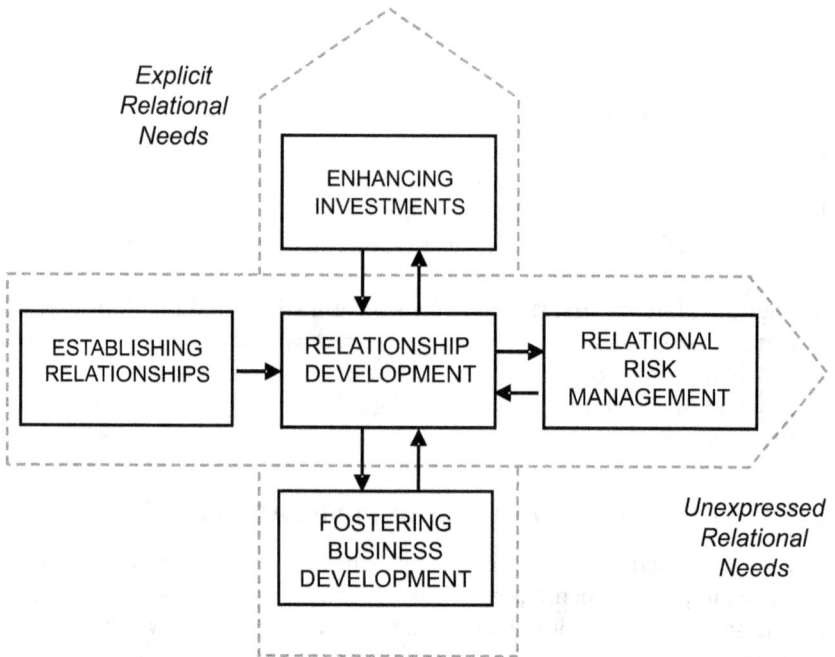

Figure 1.2 The five basic processes of public affairs.

Let's analyze each individual process to identify them in any business reality:

- **Enhancing Investments** (see Section 3.1): the premise is that for a company to maximize the effectiveness and efficiency of its core activities, it must engage with a public entity. This refers to institutional actions aimed at improving productive variables, giving them the broadest interpretative meaning possible. For example, the issuance of a regulation aimed at simplifying an implementation process may be the result of this activity.
- **Fostering Business Development** (see Section 3.2): institutional relationships facilitate the creation of a fertile environment for revenue generation, which can directly or indirectly come from public entities. All actions are carried out in full compliance with regulations governing public-private relationships. An important example is the enactment of a law that opens a new market or revitalizes an existing one by introducing incentives, providing for direct public procurement, or adjusting an existing process.
- **Establishing Relationships** (see Section 3.3): this process leads to the beginning of a relationship. It involves studying the interlocutor, making

initial contact, and laying the foundations for future interactions. The activity includes a preliminary analysis of the institutional stakeholder in terms of political objectives, operational methods, role within the governmental framework, and relationship network. It also involves organizing the meeting, which must be carefully planned.

- **Relationship Development** (see Section 3.3): developing the relationship means nurturing and strengthening it to ensure the achievement of a medium to long-term strategic objective. This phase is particularly delicate, as it assumes that there will soon be a need to engage with the identified stakeholder, yet the specific requirements are not yet fully defined. The complexity of the process lies in the need to establish a relationship despite the absence of a clearly defined objective.
- **Relational Risk Management** (see Section 3.4): this process aims to ensure the continuity of institutional dialogue even in the presence of criticalities between the institution and the company. It involves monitoring the actions of key actors and the broader context to identify and address any decisions or changes that could jeopardize the institutional relationship. This process is successful when the critical issue between the company and the institution is contained, while preserving the relationship and ensuring constructive dialogue on other matters as well.

Box 1.1 places lobbying within the context of the model described in Figure 1.2.

Box 1.1   Where does lobbying fit within the core public affairs process model?

Lobbying, primarily understood as an action aimed at influencing a regulatory production process, falls under *Enhancing Investments* or *Fostering Business Development*, depending on the specific objective to be achieved. In the managerial interpretation of PA, **lobbying represents one of the activities that can be carried out** to achieve a desired outcome. This perspective on lobbying highlights the full significance of PA as a corporate discipline, which leverages various tools and strategies, including lobbying in its strictest sense.

  For the sake of completeness, we should also ask: where does Advocacy fit? Advocacy can be employed across all processes, except for *Establishing Relationships*, where its role is generally marginal, except in certain cases where an Advocacy initiative is strategically launched before the first contact with the stakeholder.

1.3   Definitions and Simplifications

1.3.1   Organization Chart

Throughout the text, we will refer to an organizational chart that high-lights the business functions most relevant to PA activities (see Figure 1.3).

Across different contexts, similar functions may be referred to by differ-ent names, and any list would inevitably be non-exhaustive. However, offering a clear interpretative framework is sufficient to make sense of the organizational structure within one's own company. Specifically:

- The **Top Management** should include the company's CEO and any other positions with the highest authority to make strategic decisions.
- All activities related to production or the execution of the company's core business can be grouped under **Technical Functions**.
- Functions related to all stages of revenue generation should be included in **Business Functions**.
- **Other Line Functions** encompass all other operational functions.
- **Other Staff Functions** encompass all departments working for the company's internal operations and functioning.

1.3.2   Reference Technologies

In Chapter 4, "Digital Tools," we explore the instruments of **Digital Public Affairs** (hereafter **DPA**). As in other sections, we adopt a simplified approach to emphasize the functional dimensions of the digital technolo-gies employed in this domain, both in terms of internal operations (back office) and external engagement.

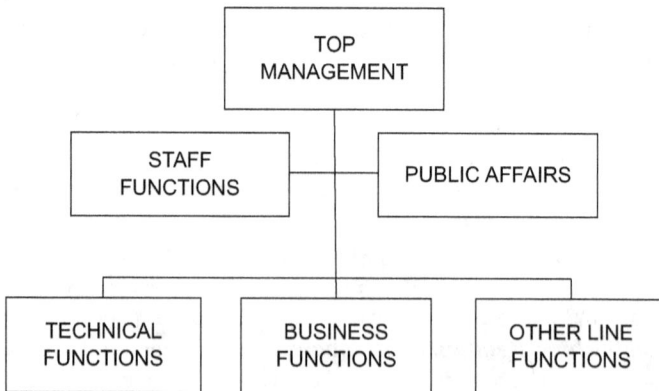

Figure 1.3 Simplified company organization chart.

- **Legacy:** the term legacy refers to all IT platforms that a PA function may use to store, analyze, and process data and information of any type and format. For the purposes of our analysis, it does not matter whether these platforms are hosted on company servers, in the cloud, or which programming languages they use. Artificial intelligence does not fall into this category, as it represents a distinct class of technology. The algorithms and capabilities that characterize AI go beyond the operational support typically provided by traditional digital platforms. For this reason, AI is considered separately in our model: its added value lies not only in increased productivity but also in enabling entirely new forms of analysis and processes.

- **Social:** the term Social encompasses all existing social networks, which are online services that enable the creation of virtual social networks and allow users to create profiles and share multimedia content. When referring to social networks in the text, we include all existing platforms, such as X, Facebook, LinkedIn, Instagram, TikTok, YouTube, etc.

- **Web:** this category includes all forms of online presence optimized for access across different devices. It encompasses a wide range of websites – whether institutional, personal, corporate, commercial, or academic – as well as platforms dedicated to news dissemination, such as newspapers and magazines. Also included are blogs of all kinds and proprietary pages managed by politicians, influencers, subject-matter experts, and other public figures, which serve as vehicles for personal or strategic expression.

- **Chat:** this term encompasses synchronous and asynchronous forms of real-time text and multimedia messaging. Some examples of solutions falling under this category, although not exhaustive, are: WhatsApp, WeChat, Telegram, Signal, etc. These systems are primarily used on mobile devices, especially smartphones, but there may also be forms of dialogue on private networks.

- **email:** email is one of the most established and widely used work tools, primarily in professional environments, both as mobile apps and in its original form on personal computers. It continues to play a significant role in institutional relations and is used daily. This category also includes newsletters of any kind, generated indiscriminately based on a subject's contacts or targeted mailing lists, produced by any actor using any available technology.

- **Artificial Intelligence** (hereafter referred to as **AI**): in recent years, the use of AI has been rapidly developing across all economic sectors and tools of this type are also being employed in institutional relations. These are mainly multi-purpose tools (Open AI, Google Gemini, Microsoft Copilot, etc.) used to implement process components typical of PA activities. Section 4.8 provides an overview of the current, evolving, and prospective uses of AI in PA, while in all other chapters, it is highlighted which tools can benefit from AI.

Notes

1 Source: Treccani Dictionary - https://www.treccani.it/vocabolario/lobby/.
2 Source: *Treccani* Dictionary - https://www.treccani.it/vocabolario/ricerca/ advocacy/.

Bibliography

Di Giacomo G., *Institutional Marketing & Public Affairs: Managing Institutional Relations to Create Value for the Business*, Franco Angeli Editore, Milan (Italy), 2019.

Gelak D., *Lobbying and Advocacy: Winning Strategies, Resources, Recommendations, Ethics and Ongoing Compliance for Lobbyists and Washington Advocates*, TheCapitol.Net, Inc., Alexandria (Virginia), 2008.

Turban E., Pollard C., Wood G., *Information Technology for Management: Driving Digital Transformation to Increase Local and Global Performance, Growth and Sustainability*, Wiley, Hoboken (New Jersey), 2023.

Chapter 2

Analysis Tools

2.1 Create the Institutional Stakeholder Profile

Understanding your institutional counterpart is of utmost importance in PA. At the beginning of the relationship, adequate time should be dedicated to analyzing the counterpart, relying primarily on three types of information sources: public information, internal company data, and insights from individuals who interact with them. This process of gathering and systematically updating the political profile of the relevant stakeholder must be carried out throughout the entire life cycle of the relationship.

The information related to a public figure will certainly be numerous and it is advisable to systematize them to facilitate their use and updating. To this end, we create the **Institutional Stakeholder Profile (ISP)**. The ISP is composed of the following sections.

2.1.1 Personal Information

The **minimum information** to gather includes the person's name, address, contact information, administrative identifiers, and digital communication channels used (websites, social networks, email, etc.). The same approach applies when dealing with an institution (rather than an individual).

2.1.2 Relationships with the Company

This section captures the company's interactions and position concerning the specific institution. It involves both quantitative and qualitative aspects that change over time. The first part of this section should provide a **summary of the commercial situation** (if applicable to the subject) using key indicators and supporting information. If the subject is a portfolio, the ISP should track the revenue trends of recent years, ongoing business negotiations, financial relationships (credits, payments, timelines, etc.).

The second part of this section is dedicated to the **technical position of the subject** in relation to the company's operational scope. It includes the

DOI: 10.4324/9781003647829-3

regulations and projects of the administration that have an impact on the company. It is essential to understand a stakeholder's political stance in relation to a specific area of interest.

The third and final part focuses on **existing critical issues** with the interlocutor. It not only highlights commercial and technical problems but also encompasses other aspects such as legal, administrative, and employment-related issues. This aspect is examined in detail in Section 3.4.

2.1.3   Public Affairs Interventions

The section summarizes important PA actions that have been carried out toward the public entity in the recent past, are currently ongoing, and are planned for the future.

2.1.4   Contact Register

Another important data point to monitor is the set of interactions between any company representative and the institution, which should be systematically recorded in the *Contact Register*. Maintaining this register requires establishing effective communication with personnel from other departments who manage such relationships, often of a commercial nature.

The Contact Register includes the following **information:**

- **Institutional Contact Details:** name and role of the person met.
- **Record of Interactions:** a log of significant meetings between the contact person and company representatives, including dates, participants, topics discussed, and key outcomes.
- **Subjective Notes:** a brief qualitative assessment of the contact's attitude toward the company.

2.1.5   Status of the Public Subject

This refers primarily to the ability of the actor – whether an individual or an institution – to effectively exercise their role at a given point in time (see Table 2.2).

2.1.6   Strategic Position

This section presents key strategic indicators that define the company's relationship with the institution. A detailed explanation of these indicators is provided in Chapter 5, "Strategic Tools." The indicators to be reported include: the *Importance of the Relationship* (γ), its *Difficulty* (δ), its *Risk Index* (ρ), the expected *Business Impact* (b), and the expected *Technical Impact* (t), all quantified monetarily. Additionally, the subject's classification within the *Institutional Positioning Matrix* should be highlighted (see Figure 5.2).

2.1.7 Essential Documentation

The ISP may include attachments limited to relevant documents that characterize the active relationships with the institution.

Figure 2.1 provides a graphical example of an ISP.

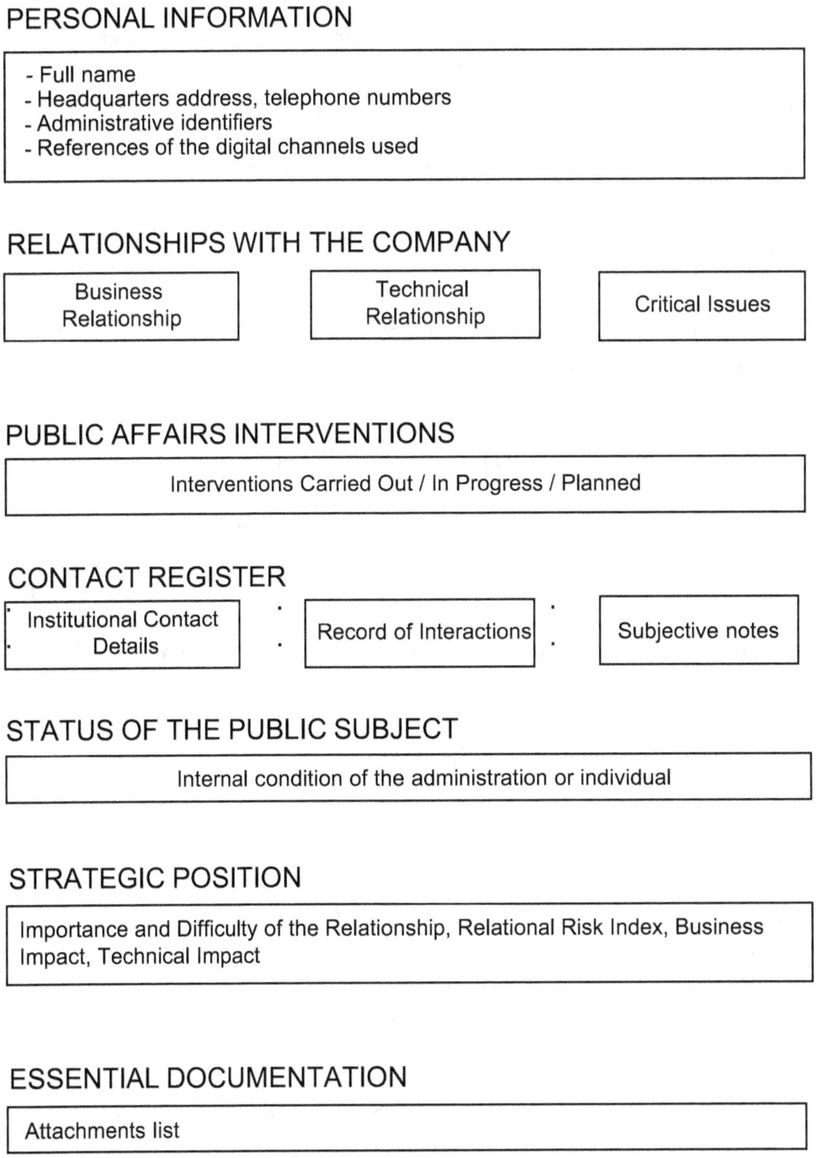

PERSONAL INFORMATION

- Full name
- Headquarters address, telephone numbers
- Administrative identifiers
- References of the digital channels used

RELATIONSHIPS WITH THE COMPANY

| Business Relationship | Technical Relationship | Critical Issues |

PUBLIC AFFAIRS INTERVENTIONS

Interventions Carried Out / In Progress / Planned

CONTACT REGISTER

| Institutional Contact Details | Record of Interactions | Subjective notes |

STATUS OF THE PUBLIC SUBJECT

Internal condition of the administration or individual

STRATEGIC POSITION

Importance and Difficulty of the Relationship, Relational Risk Index, Business Impact, Technical Impact

ESSENTIAL DOCUMENTATION

Attachments list

Figure 2.1 Institutional stakeholder profile.

2.2   Draw the Institutional Relationship Map

The *Institutional Relationship Map* is one of the core tools in PA activities. It provides a schematic representation of the key relationships that a public entity is presumed to maintain with other institutions, intermediaries, companies, associations, and similar actors. Constructing the map requires identifying these actors and the nature of the relationships they are assumed to have with the policymaker.

The criteria for including a public actor in the map may vary, as the entities involved often pursue different objectives and fulfill distinct roles. Importantly, the number of attributes or connections an actor displays should not be the sole determinant of their relevance. In some cases, even a single defining characteristic may be sufficient for an actor to exert a pivotal influence.

Let's explore the key characteristics that make a public subject relevant for PA, these include:

- **Institutional Relevance:** we need to understand a subject's political weight at a given moment, meaning its ability to influence strategic and political decisions. As we will see in Section 5.1, institutional relevance is one of the key determinants of the relationship's importance.
- **Technical Relevance:** it refers to the subject's ability to modify the operational context through regulatory or normative actions. The introduction of new reference standards is also a prerogative of these actors.
- **Business Relevance:** this factor measures both the public entity's ability to allocate economic resources for future public investments and the likelihood that it belongs to a public administration that is a client of our company.

We now introduce the figure of the **Intermediary**, a key player in the world of PA.

The intermediary can be a public or private entity that engages in dialogue with businesses and institutions, facilitating discussions and often expressing positions on specific issues. This role is based on their disciplinary expertise; their position within the economic, political, and social context; and their ability to represent the common interests of multiple stakeholders.

The **most common types of intermediaries** include:

- **Associations:** groups of private, public, or mixed entities that come together based on shared interests, sector affiliation, or geographical location.

- **Experts:** individuals with recognized authority in their field, typically affiliated with universities, research centers, leading consultancy firms, or highly accredited professionals.
- **Entities with Specific Purposes:** such as political parties, foundations, non-governmental organizations, local movements, and similar organizations.
- **Think Tank:** research-oriented organizations that produce policy analyses and recommendations to inform public debate and influence decision-making processes.

Intermediaries must be carefully considered when designing the *Map*. Generally, *Think Tanks* are not included, as their ability to exert direct influence on institutions regarding specific business issues is marginal. However, they may play a more significant role in Advocacy activities, particularly those of a long-term nature.

Just like institutions, intermediaries have **key attributes** that must be assessed to understand their effectiveness and role at a given time, in relation to a specific issue, and in connection with certain institutions.

The factors to analyze in order to qualify an intermediary are:

- **Representativeness:** this attribute is typical of associations and expresses their ability to aggregate relevant actors in the context and define common positions to represent. An association that brings together, for example, the most relevant companies in a sector has a high level of representation.
- **Excellence:** this is an objective factor for both an individual and an organization. The most classic actors distinguished by excellence are universities and consequently, professors and researchers.
- **Uniqueness:** uniqueness should not be confused with excellence. It does not evaluate the competence of the subject but acknowledges the exclusive possession of a characteristic. A unique expertise linked to a patent or the privileged trust relationship between an actor and a policymaker is an example of the heterogeneity of uniqueness.
- **Pervasiveness:** it is the ability to reach the highest number of relevant subjects possible. It is typical of **influencers** and authoritative experts in the industry who employ both traditional and digital channels.

Now we **assign an intensity to the identified attributes,** meaning we evaluate the subjects based on their responsibilities and the activities they should perform. Table 2.1 facilitates the assignment of intensities. Similar tables can be defined based on specific contexts, focusing on a primary indicator or using a secondary one to ensure that no subjects of interest are eliminated.

Table 2.1 Attribute Intensity of Institutions and Intermediaries

	High (3)	Medium (2)	Low (1)	None (0)
Institutional Relevance	It defines the regulatory framework of the sector	It defines the regulatory framework for a specific domain	It influences the regulatory environment	It does not have a significant impact on the company or its operational environment
Technical Relevance	It determines the technical framework within which the industry operates	It defines only a limited set of technical aspects	It exerts influence over technical decision-making	It does not have a technical impact on the company or its operational context
Business Relevance	It is an important customer or directly manages significant resources	It is a customer of medium interest	It is a customer of little interest	It is not of business interest
Representativeness	It represents a significant number of entities	It represents a specific set of needs	It is active in a tightly circumscribed sector-specific field	It represents a small number of actors
Excellence	It serves as a benchmark within the operational context	The high value of the service is broadly recognized	Excellence exists in domains of secondary importance to the company	Any excellence present does not influence the operational context
Uniqueness	It has a unique attribute directly related to company's business	It holds a distinctive feature with an indirect connection to the business activity	Its uniqueness holds little relevance to the company's operational scope	Its uniqueness is not relevant to the company
Pervasiveness	It reaches all stakeholders relevant to the company	It reaches a significant share of the company's key stakeholders	It engages only a limited class of actors of interest to the company	It does not reach a sufficient number of relevant stakeholders

For very large companies, completing the table can be quite complex; therefore, it can be useful to **define a focused analysis perimeter**. The variables that can be used to circumscribe the analysis are:

- **Geographical:** this is the classic territorial delimitation. It is recommended to start with the national context and identify subjects that operate centrally and have an impact on the territory.
- **Sectoral:** if the company operates across multiple sectors, a dedicated analysis should be carried out for each. Where sub-sectors involve distinct institutional counterparts, preparing multiple grids may again prove useful.
- **Functional:** it may be advisable to define the perimeter of the analysis based on the operational scope of different company divisions. If no significant differences emerge, it is preferable to avoid duplicating the analysis unnecessarily.
- **Thematic:** if the company plans to undertake a project focused on a specific theme, a dedicated analysis may be appropriate. To minimize the risk of error, it is advisable to start with an extensive grid that can be progressively refined as needed.

To further **narrow the field of observation,** multiple variables can be combined. It is common to circumscribe the analysis by both country and sector. Visualizing the defined perimeter graphically can be particularly helpful (see Figure 2.2). Each state, of course, has its own administrative structures, which may include various levels of decentralization. However, it is generally possible to identify distinct layers of government, ranging from local or municipal levels to national and international ones. Figure 2.2 can be applied to any country by simply renaming the government levels as appropriate.

2.2.1 Evaluation of the Effectiveness of Institutions and Intermediaries

We have just introduced the main attributes to assess in an institution or an intermediary. Now, let's try to understand, through detailed variables, **whether these actors are truly capable of performing the role assigned to them.** The priorities, operational methods, and effectiveness of their actions are linked to the political and managerial choices made by top figures. As a result, the actual role and effectiveness of the actor can significantly vary over time. Therefore, we need to understand how actors have interpreted their assigned role and what strategy they have designed.

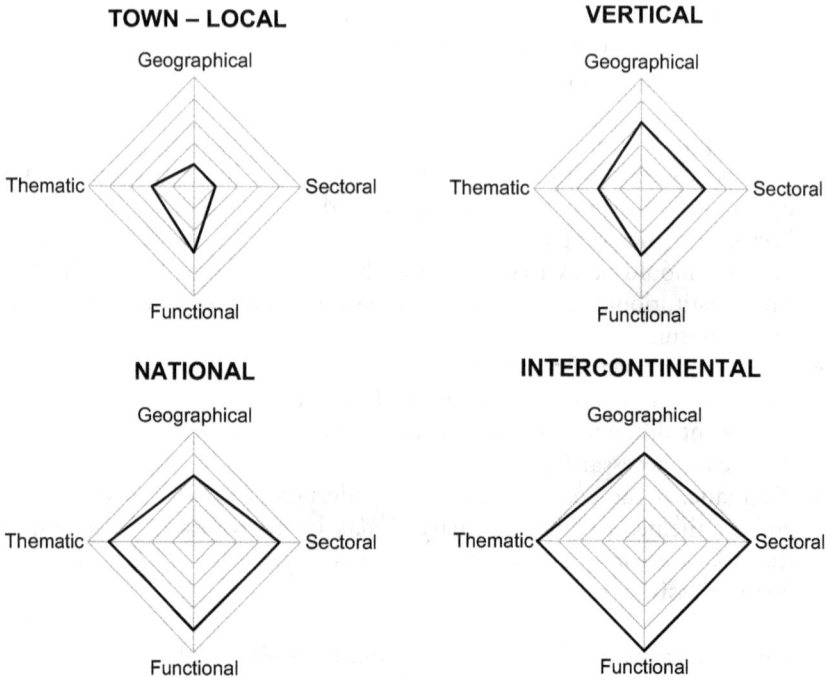

Figure 2.2 Perimeter of analysis of the interlocutors.

Let's identify the elements to analyze for each actor:

- **Priorities:** it is crucial to know which issues have been given priority to understand the actual relevance assigned to those of our interest.
- **Capacity:** it refers to the ability to have all the material and immaterial factors necessary to ensure the execution of actions required to achieve the identified objectives.
- **Stability:** a subject is considered stable if it can ensure continuity in the execution of an activity even when internal or external factors modify its strategy or operational structure.
- **Effectiveness:** it is the ability to achieve results and is perhaps the most significant attribute of all, assuming that all the other attributes are present.

For the analysis of **Intermediaries' roles,** we use two additional attributes:

- **Reliability:** it is the degree of trust assigned to the subject based on the existing relationship, the people who compose it, and how it is perceived by institutions.
- **Availability:** it is the actual willingness to collaborate with our company and depends on various factors.

Tables 2.2 and 2.3 display the elements for evaluating the listed factors, and in some cases, they are broken down into their components. These tables can be easily associated with an algorithm capable of providing

Table 2.2 Framework for Analyzing the Role of Institutions

#	Factors	Assessment
1	Priority	Priority list
2	Capacity	Adequate, Partially Adequate, Not Adequate + Note
2.1	Institutional Strength	High, Medium, Low
2.1.1	Position held	Primary or Secondary
2.1.2	Scope of delegated Authority	Strong or Medium
2.1.3	Political provenance	Strong, Medium, Weak
2.1.4	Government objectives	Objectives List
2.2	Skills	Total, Partial, Null
2.2.1	Process-based work	Adequate, Inadequate
2.2.2	Technical skills	Adequate, Not Adequate

(Continued)

Table 2.2 (Continued)

#	Factors	Assessment
2.3	**Context**	**Positive, Neutral, Negative**
2.3.1	Economic and social situation	Positive, Neutral, Negative
2.3.2	Stakeholder's support	Positive, Negative
2.3.4	Technical initiative sharing	Positive, Negative
2.4	**Financial resources**	**Consistent, Medium, Modest**
3	**Stability**	**Highly Likely, Likely, Unlikely**
3.1	Political continuity	Likely, Unlikely
3.2	Responsiveness of the structure	High Low
3.3	Recognized usefulness	Recognized, Not Recognized
3.3.1	Specific sector	Relevant, Not Relevant
3.3.2	Action type	Consistent (...), Little Consistent (...)
3.3.3	Nature of usefulness	Evident (...), Not Evident
3.4	**Degree of Commitment**	**(Variable) Large, Medium, Small**
3.5	**Disapproval**	**High, Medium, Low**
3.5.1	Impartial criticisms	Consistent, Inconsistent
3.5.2	Opinion-based criticisms	Very Consistent, Consistent, Not Consistent
4	**Effectiveness**	**High, Medium, Low**
4.1	**Program clarity**	**Complete, Partial, Deficient**
4.1.1	Strategy	Consistent, inconsistent
4.1.2	Goals	Consistent, Inconsistent
4.1.3	Actions	Consistent, Inconsistent
4.1.4	Organization	Consistent, inconsistent
4.1.5	Financial aspects	Consistent, Inconsistent
4.1.6	Consistency	Consistent, inconsistent
4.2	**Consistency of results**	**Consistent, inconsistent**
4.2.1	Numerousness	Consistent, inconsistent
4.2.2	Concreteness	Consistent, inconsistent
4.3	**Traceability of results**	**High, Partial, Nothing**
4.3.1	Transparency	High, Medium, Absent
4.3.2	Precision	High, Medium, Low
4.4	**Willingness to improve**	**High Low**

Table 2.3 Framework for Analyzing the role of Intermediaries

#	Factors	Assessment
1	**Priority**	**Consistent, Doubtful + List**
1.1	**Consistency and Clarity**	**Punctual, Ambiguous**
1.2	**Ethics**	**Flawless, Ordinary, Doubtful**
2	**Capacity**	**Adequate, Partially Adequate, Not Adequate + Note**
2.1	**Relevance of the Entity**	**High, Moderate, Low**
2.1.1	Position in the context	Primary, Secondary
2.1.2	Scope of the entity	Strong, Medium, Weak
2.2	**Institution's Perception of Relevance**	**Significant, Limited, Marginal**
2.3	**Skills**	**Total, Partial, Null**
2.3.1	Process-based work	Adequate, Inadequate
2.3.2	Technical skills	Adequate, Not Adequate
2.4	**Context**	**Favorable, Uncertain, Unfavorable**
2.4.1	Support from direct stakeholders	Consistent, Formal, Poor
2.4.2	Support from institutions	Obvious, Doubtful, Unclassifiable
3	**Stability**	**Highly Likely, Likely, Unlikely**
3.1	Management continuity	Likely, Unlikely
3.2	Recognized usefulness	Negotiator, Organizer, Excellence, Achievement, None
3.3	Economic consistency	Solid, Doubtful, Not Applicable
4	**Effectiveness**	**High, Medium, Low**
4.1	**Program clarity**	**Complete, Partial, Deficient**
4.1.1	Strategy – Objectives – Actions	Consistent, inconsistent
4.1.2	Organization	Consistent, inconsistent
4.2	**Consistency of results**	**Consistent, inconsistent**
4.2.1	Enumerability	Consistent, inconsistent
4.2.2	Concreteness	Consistent, inconsistent
4.3	**Willingness to improve**	**High Low**
5	**Reliability**	**Total, Partial, Not Detectable**
5.1	**Objective reliability**	**Total, Partial, Not Detectable**
5.1.1	Seriousness	Total, Partial, Not Detectable
5.1.2	Transparency	Total, Partial, Nothing

(Continued)

Table 2.3 (Continued)

#	Factors	Assessment
5.2	**Perceived Reliability**	**Total, Partial, Not Detectable**
5.2.1	Direct experience	Positive, Negative, Not Evaluable
5.2.2	Guarantees	Consistent, Inconsistent
6	**Availability**	**High, Ordinary, Modest**
6.1	Consideration	High, Ordinary, Modest
6.2	Involvement	Elevated, Ordinary, Modest
6.3	Critical Barriers	Absent, Present

quantitative evaluations to facilitate comparisons and enhance understanding of the effectiveness and role of the actors. AI tools are well-suited for this activity.

To evaluate these parameters, we undoubtedly need to gather information that is not always available on the web. Naturally, we will need to interpret the data we collect, and here AI can be helpful, but often we must rely on our intuition to correlate aspects that come from different sources, including unwritten ones. The suggestion is to evaluate only the parameters for which we have reasonable certainty of being correct.

A second, and even more important, recommendation is this: **be courageous in our assessments for the good of the company.** Let us clarify this point. The reader will have noticed that some variables – whether applied to institutions or intermediaries – can, in certain cases, reveal that a subject is not capable of effectively fulfilling its role. It is important to recognize and clearly state this when it occurs. Failing to do so would mean building PA initiatives on assumptions about capabilities that, in reality, are not demonstrated or acted upon. These tables, therefore, not only help us design the *Institutional Relationship Map* (see Figure 2.3) but also serve as an essential tool for planning our activities with accuracy.

2.2.2 Actions of Institutions and Intermediaries

So far, we have outlined a static scenario where each entity plays a role based on its characteristics. Now, we will explore the dynamics by analyzing the various types of actions performed by the actors.

The **main actions** that can be carried out are:

- **Decides:** this is the role of the decision-maker, unequivocally the most important actor. Typically, this is a top-level institutional figure, although it may also be a subject delegated by them.
- **Represents the decision:** this is responsibility of the official decision-maker, who is accountable for communicating the decision.

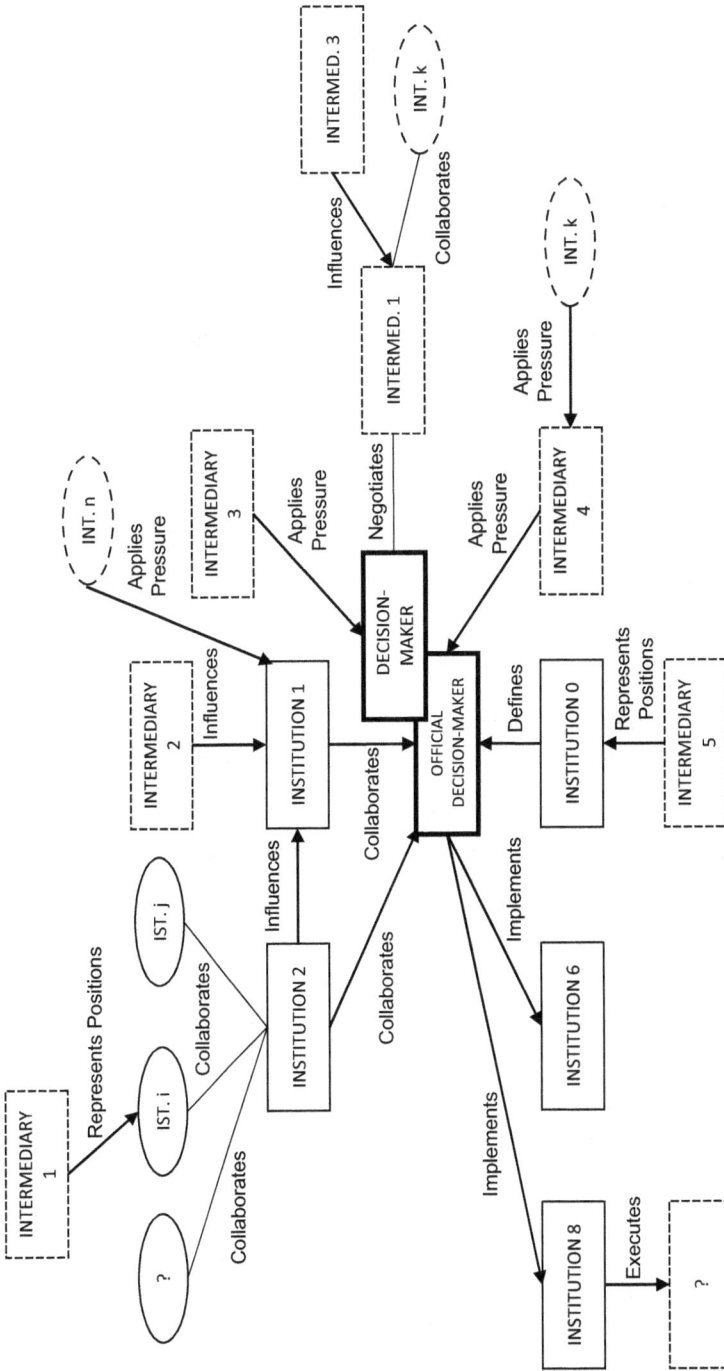

Figure 2.3 Institutional relationship map.

- **Collaborates** (with the decision-maker): the decision-maker may have official collaborators or may informally involve others who actively participate in the decision-making process.
- **Defines:** an institution can set the contextual rules, shaping or influencing the actions of other public actors, primarily through normative actions.
- **Influences:** this refers to the ability of one entity to shape or guide the choices of another.
- **Negotiates:** this is the typical role of an actor tasked with reaching an agreement with the decision-maker or their staff.
- **Exerts Pressure:** pressure can be applied to the decision-maker to influence them toward a particular choice.
- **Represents Positions:** typically, intermediaries express the positions of the entities they represent.
- **Implements:** the implementer is the actor who translates the decision-maker's choices into operational actions, managing all the technical tasks that precede and enable the actual implementation phase.
- **Executes:** this refers to the actor who physically carries out the activities defined in the operational plan.

At this point, we have all the qualifying elements to describe an institution and an intermediary, also in terms of actions they can undertake at a specific moment in a given context. Table 2.4 presents an example of a concise profile sheet for an institution and an intermediary; a simplified representation of the evaluation of attributes (both static and dynamic) has been adopted, using a scale based on the number of "+" signs. As the number of "+" signs increases, the attribute is present and denotes a significant intensity. The tables seen earlier (Tables 2.1, 2.2, and 2.3), if properly utilized, can provide more detailed evaluations of the attributes presented in Table 2.4.

2.2.3 Graphic Representation of the Institutional Relationship Map

As we have seen, the Map can be drawn with reference to a specific actor or need, and it provides valuable input both during the definition of the PA strategy and throughout the implementation of actions in the field. It is essential that this document is constantly updated to ensure that initiatives are directed toward interlocutors who actually hold the identified roles. The tool is also crucial for coordinating institutional actions with the technical and commercial activities carried out by the relevant functions that interact with the same stakeholders.

Table 2.4 Static Profile and Dynamic Profile

INSTITUTION i			
Static Profile		**Dynamic Profile**	
Relevance	**Rating**	**Actions**	**Rating**
Institutional Relevance	+++	Decides	
Technical Relevance	++	Represents decision	
Business Relevance	+	Collaborates (with the decision-maker)	++
Role	**Rating**	Defines (orients)	
Priority	++	Influences	
Capacity	+++	Represents position	
Stability	+	Implements	
Effectiveness	++		
INTERMEDIARY j			
STATIC PROFILE		**DYNAMIC PROFILE**	
Relevance	**Rating**	**Actions**	**Rating**
Representativeness	++	Collaborates (with the decision-maker)	
Excellence		Influences	
Uniqueness		Negotiates	
Pervasiveness		Applies pressure	
Role	**Rating**	Represents positions	++
Priority	+	Implements	
Capacity	++	Executes	
Stability	+++		
Effectiveness	+		
Reliability	+		
Availability	++		

Now, we introduce the **graphic conventions** for designing the Map:

- **Entity** representation: rectangle.
- **Person** representation: ellipse.
- **Institution:** rectangles with solid borders; the official decision-maker has a bold solid border.
- **Intermediary:** rectangles with dashed borders.
- **Person in an Institution:** an ellipse with a solid border.
- **Person in an Intermediary role:** an ellipse with a dashed border.

- **Connectors:**
  - *Solid lines with an arrowhead terminal* indicate an action from ... to ...
  - *Dashed lines* represent uncertain actions by the active subject.
  - *Lines without terminals* indicate no direct action.
- **Actions:** displayed in abbreviated text format near the corresponding connectors.
- **Decision-Maker Placement:** positioned at the center of the diagram.
- **Repetition for clarity:** An actor may appear multiple times within the Map for visual clarity.
- **Connecting Multiple Maps:** a numbered circle, reached by a connector, links different maps.
- **Unknown Recipients:** if the recipient institution/intermediary of an action is unknown, a question mark is inserted in the box.

Figure 2.3 presents an example of a Map constructed for a hypothetical case, illustrating the final result. The boxes should be arranged as systematically as possible to enhance readability, minimizing repetition of subjects. In practice, real Maps can range from very simple to highly complex. In the latter case, it is advisable to consider breaking them down into multiple Maps for clarity. Naturally, AI tools can be useful both for gathering information to populate the Map and for representing and updating it.

2.3   Identify Digital Relationships

Let's take a moment to define **Web, Social, and Media (hereinafter referred to as WSM) actions,** highlighting the aspects that are relevant from a DPA perspective. **A WSM action can be defined as any digital communication carried out by actors within the PA system and their stakeholders.** The main actors naturally include institutions, intermediaries, and businesses, while stakeholders – whether individually or collectively – can be the recipients of an initiative, entities entitled to express an opinion, or third-party actors. The virtual manifestation of a WSM action can take various forms, such as a text or multimedia post, a video (speech, interview, commentary, etc.), a reel or an instant message (direct, within a community, as part of a discussion thread, etc.). The most common types of content include expressions of intent, approval, dissent, rebuttals of positions, representation of stances or arguments, promotion of facts or situations, in-depth analyses, and debates on specific issues. This category also encompasses the crucial class of journalistic content published on any digital platform that relates to the institutional matters under consideration.

Similarly to the physical world in which we have always been accustomed to operating, we must learn to interpret the **relationships** between actors in the public and private sectors **within the digital universe.** These relationships must be characterized by a dedicated system of attributes, which allow us to highlight the behaviors we expect from these actors in the virtual arena.

In the realm of DPA, there is a corresponding representation of the *Institutional Relationship Map* (Figure 2.3), which incorporates actors and their online interactions. This representation is known as the **Web, Social, and Media Relationship Map. The WSM Relationship Map illustrates the digital activities and engagements of the identified actors.**

The **actors we will position on the Map** include: institutions, associations, experts, and universities (in this case, the category of intermediaries has been broken down into its three most representative actors), businesses, individuals (involved in the digital web of relationships in any capacity), influencers (whose specific role in DPA will be explored in Section 4.3), and communities (groups of actors of any kind who share the same position on a given issue). Figure 2.4 represents an example of a WSM Relationship Map constructed with a relevant policymaker at the center.

We **categorize the actions** that actors can undertake as follows:

- **Favorable:** these are all the WSM actions that support the position of the central subject. This prediction is based on the historical analysis of actors' behaviors, taking into account all relevant aspects to qualify a future intervention.
- **Unpredictable:** the subject is characterized by low consistency in their actions and generally takes varying positions of support or opposition depending on the theme.
- **Adverse:** these are actions that are symmetrically opposed to the favorable ones.

We introduce the actions conducted by a Community, which are WSM manifestations carried out by individuals belonging to homogeneous clusters that can have mainly two natures:

- **Permanent:** these are subjects who are consistently united by an attribute, such as belonging to a political party, an association, etc.
- **Temporary:** these are actors who aggregate based on a specific project or shared objective.

The identified subjects may exhibit strong hostility or support, but they can also take on ambiguous roles with low consistency.

In the WSM Map, we also consider both the **likelihood of an action** occurring and its **potential intensity.** While these two factors are closely related, they can have distinct values.

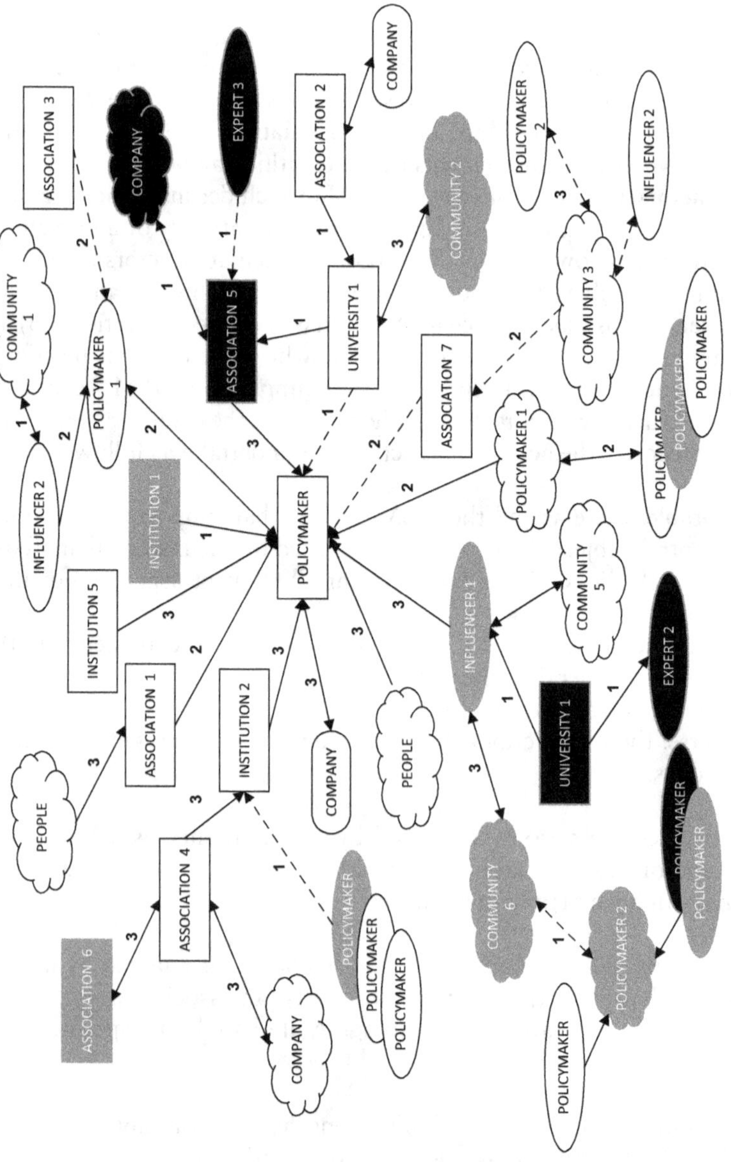

Figure 2.4 Web, social, and media relationship map.

Likelihood addresses the question: is the actor likely to engage in WSM actions on a specific issue?

Intensity reflects how frequently or forcefully we anticipate the WSM campaign will unfold if the subject chooses to participate.

Intensity can be measured on a scale from 1 to 3, while Likelihood will be classified as High or Low.

Another key factor to consider is the **Reciprocity of supportive or offensive actions** between two actors. Intuitively, one might assume that if a subject has expressed support for another, the latter would be inclined to return the favor. However, this is not always the case in practice. Identifying when and why this reciprocity occurs can provide valuable insights into the virtual profile and behavioral patterns of the actor in question.

Let's systematize the introduced elements for a comprehensive representation (Figure 2.4) and provide a reasoned legend, in detail:

- Generally active actors on the theme/territory:

  - *Our operating company*: rectangle with rounded corners.
  - *Institutions/organizations*: rectangle.
  - *Individuals* (politicians, experts, influencers, etc.): ellipse.
  - *Communities* (associated with an entity, followers, etc.): cloud.

- Expected position of the actor:

  - *Favorable*: white background of the figure.
  - *Unpredictable*: gray background of the figure.
  - *Adverse*: black background of the figure.

- Probability of the actor carrying out a WSM action on the theme:

  - *High probability*: solid line.
  - *Low probability*: dashed line.

- Expected intensity of the intervention:

  - *High*: number 3 represented on the line.
  - *Medium*: number 2 represented on the line.
  - *Low*: number 1 represented on the line.
  - *Unpredictable*: no number.

- Reciprocity of intervention:

  - *Reciprocity*: arrow with tips at both ends.
  - *Non-reciprocity*: arrow with a tip pointing in the direction of the actor performing the action toward the other.
  - *Unpredictable*: no tip/arrow at the end.

By using dedicated digital platforms, multidimensional analyses can be performed, integrating actors, timelines, projects, information, etc., and carrying out elaborations that would be unthinkable manually.

In this case, we can make more advanced use of AI, going beyond mere data systematization by leveraging **generative AI** to hypothesize digital and forward-looking relationships among the considered actors and potentially identify new ones. Naturally, the system must be properly trained to generate credible hypotheses, which should still undergo further traditional analysis.

2.4   Analyze Hidden Relationships and Shadow Communications

Real-time information sharing with selected groups of actors is a powerful tool for supporting advocacy efforts, enabled by the combination of instant messaging and the widespread use of smartphones. In some cases, messages can spread within minutes, reaching target interlocutors who would otherwise ignore communications from untrusted groups or individuals.

Strategically activated groups can generate significant waves of likes and comments on shared posts, amplifying their visibility. The activation patterns of these groups and the management of feedback present intriguing dynamics. Theoretically, **one can map out intricate networks of shadow communication running parallel to the public evolution of a thread.**

This technique plays a key role in shaping public perception, whether of a figure (increasingly political) or of a position or proposal. While this phenomenon is extensively covered in literature on social communication, our focus here is on the use of WhatsApp groups and similar tools for PA purposes.

It is particularly convenient to design this map by starting with a key actor placed at the center of the scheme. The choice of this figure depends on the objective we are pursuing, the guiding question, and the specific domain we are working on in terms of DPA.

AI can provide valuable support in hypothesizing these types of relationships, which, unlike those in the previous two maps (see Figures 2.3 and 2.4), can branch out in a much more complex and less predictable manner. Naturally, the more reliable the analysis, the higher the chances of success for the actions undertaken.

For example, we can map the chat networks of a company's PA Chief. These include both active and potential connection. We then progressively hypothesize the cascade of channels managed by the identified interlocutors.

This exercise is illustrated in Figure 2.5, following these graphical conventions:

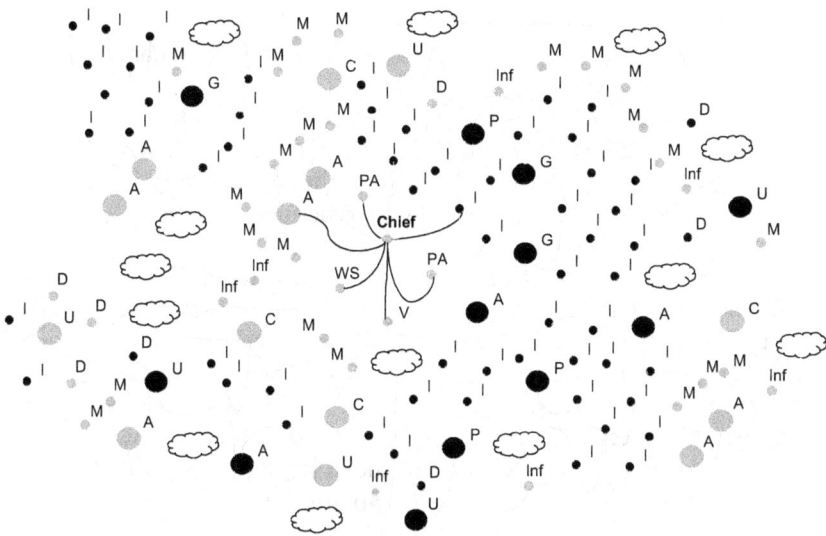

Figure 2.5 Hidden relationships.

- *Small dots*: represent individuals.
- *Large dots*: represent groups of people.
- *Black dots*: indicate public entities.
- *Gray dots*: indicate private entities.
- I: Individuals representing an institution.
- C: Companies (group chats involving multiple individuals from the same company).
- M: Individuals representing companies or similar entities.
- D: Recognized experts affiliated with universities or other authoritative institutions, possessing significant expertise in a specific field.
- A: Associations of any kind, composed of private and/or public individuals (referring to a group chat with multiple members affiliated with or delegated by associated entities).
- U: Universities or research institutions (referring to a group chat within a university involving multiple professors).
- G: Group chats of institutional actors used for various topics, not accessible to the public.
- P: Group chats shared among party members, structured at multiple levels.
- V/PA/WS: Key internal contacts of the Chief within the company, including top management (V), PA managers (PA), and web and social media communication officers (WS).

- *Inf*: Influencers and other actors operating in WSM.
- *Clouds*: Groups of varying sizes sharing the same group chat.

In Figure 2.5, the active/potential chats between some of the indicated actors are drawn with a continuous gray line. To simplify the visualization, not all existing chats have been included, as they are obviously much more numerous. It is assumed that there are no repetitions among the identified actors to avoid making the diagram unreadable.

Let's now examine the typical groups whose existence is assumed, organizing them to identify the most likely participants in each group. In addition to those previously mentioned, we introduce **three mixed groups** composed of diverse individuals who share one or more areas of interest. We categorize the participants as follows: institutional, experts, corporate, and influencers. Table 2.5 presents these actors as rows and the groups as columns. **Each cell is color-coded – white, gray, or black –** to reflect the increasing likelihood of participants' involvement in the respective groups.

Table 2.5 helps us bring order to the universe of multiple and multidimensional connections shown in Figure 2.5. We immediately observe that **institutional groups** (G, P) and **corporate groups** (C) are closed groups, where it is highly unlikely for an outsider to be admitted. This approach is based on correct principles of confidentiality and ethics, so it should not be surprising. A similar but slightly more flexible situation applies to expert groups (U), which may include institutional figures and individuals from the business sector. Finally, associations (A) are groups formed by all or part of the members and may also involve the participation of experts and individuals from companies or institutions, depending on whether they are public or private actor association groups.

However, it is important to note that direct presence of influencers is unlikely in these "pure" groups. **Influencers, in the context of DPA,** primarily serve as specific task performers and explicitly feature in mixed groups that involve heterogeneous actors.

Table 2.5 Instant Messaging Relationships between Public and Private Actors

Members	G	P	U	A	C	M1	M2	M3
Institutions	gray		gray	black		black		black
Experts			black	gray		gray	gray	
Officers (from Company)			gray	black	black		black	gray
Influencers						gray	black	gray

2.4.1 *Mixed Groups Overview*

Mixed groups (M1, M2, M3) are dynamic configurations that include both public and private actors who share a specific area of interest. In many cases, these groups may also involve recognized influencers or consultants, provided their presence is accepted by other members. While their composition can vary depending on the context, some profiles are typically expected to participate, though not all identified actors will necessarily play an active role.

M1 – Institutional Chat
Primarily composed of public actors, M1 groups also include representatives from associations of public entities and experts, particularly from academic backgrounds.
M2 – Private Chat
These groups consist mainly of private actors, extended to well-established stakeholders such as associations, foundations, and research institutions.
M3 – Project Chat
These groups bring together both public and private actors collaborating on a specific project. In complex initiatives, multiple chats may exist, but typically only one includes the most relevant figures.

Messages travel quickly and unpredictably through these direct and group virtual networks. As a result, great caution is required when sharing content. **This characteristic of instant messaging makes it comparable to a social media post.** Once sent, a message leaves our control. The recipient is part of a digital network and further sharing depends on how valuable they find the content.

On the other hand, this communication technique has the **power to deliver content directly to the pockets** of many qualified interlocutors through individuals within their relational networks, rather than from our company itself. This feature is valuable for synchronizing communication campaigns, promoting posts, and enhancing institutional credibility. By identifying the right flow, we can transmit specific content to one or more public entities via a transmission network that is perceived as both reliable and substantial.

As with other advocacy efforts, we cannot guarantee that messages will reach recipients in the desired manner or within the intended time frame. In fact, some messages may never reach the intended audience at all. To reduce this risk, we should use redundancy: activate multiple contacts to raise the chances that the message reaches its intended recipient. However, we must also be mindful of the potential for **communication overload,** although this is not quite the same as spamming, which tends to affect topics that are not a priority for the recipient, even if it originates from known sources.

In the context of groups, a key concern is the non-reading of messages in rooms that are not viewed as strategic by the public entity. Much like in daily life, there will be a tendency to prioritize content based on perceived importance.

2.5   Assessing the Potential for Institutional Relationship Development

To understand a company's potential to build relevant relationships, we will analyze the following factors: (a) Company Network, (b) Personal Network (PA staff), (c) Top Management network, (d) Company Relevance (for institutions), (e) Thematic Relevance, (f) Public Affairs techniques (and organization). Once the intensity of the individual indicators has been assessed (using a simple scale from 1 to 5), we will represent it in a dedicated diagram. This diagram provides three key pieces of information: our **Relational Potential**, its **Evolution over Time**, and our **Positioning Relative to Peers** (if we can estimate their situation). These insights must be carefully considered both when defining a strategy and implementing actions, as they serve as a measure of the quality and consistency of the PA network we can rely on.

In this case, AI is primarily used in an operational capacity. However, if we were able to develop an integrated corporate AI system, it could provide significant forecasts on the evolution of our potential network based on decisions – even those not directly related to relationships – made at the corporate or functional level.

2.5.1   Company Network

The company network is composed of stable relationships cultivated over time within the organization. Its evaluation should encompass all existing connections, regardless of the function that originally established them. This includes direct relationships with policymakers as well as key figures within governmental structures, which are crucial for ensuring continuity, particularly during political transitions.

Additionally, indirect channels to institutions – such as intermediaries – are also part of this network. Table 2.6 assigns a value to different levels of the company network, providing a structured assessment of its strength and reach.

Table 2.6 Value of the Company Network

Value	Company Network
0	**Non-existent**; typically applies to start-up companies or those that do not engage with public entities
1	**Limited**; due to the nature of the company's activities, direct relationships with policymakers are not essential and connections with key industry stakeholders are considered sufficient
2	**Vertical**; focused exclusively on institutional figures directly relevant to the company's business activities
3	**Vertical (high level) + stakeholders**; in addition to high-level sector-specific relationships, the company maintains connections with key stakeholders, though not all are actively engaged in collaboration
4	**Extensive and active**; the company maintains well-structured relationships with both institutions and key stakeholders
5	**Extensive, established, and active**; the company has established structured relationships with all relevant institutions and implements coordinated initiatives with the majority of stakeholders

2.5.2 Personal Network (PA Function)

All individuals within a PA function – whether permanent or temporary – gradually build external contacts and relationships. While tenure plays a key role in shaping personal networks, it is essential that these connections are transformed into a stable corporate asset.

To accurately assess the potential for relationship development, it is necessary to evaluate both the company's institutional network and the personal networks of individual PA staff separately. Table 2.7 assigns a value to different levels of personal networks within the PA function.

2.5.3 Top Management Network

Top management typically maintains direct relationships with policymakers; these connections form a unique subset of their personal network, often at a high level. Possessing such a network and having positive professional experiences with prominent institutional representatives is a distinctive asset found only in top executive roles. The extensive mandates held by these individuals enable them to engage with top political figures from various perspectives, whereas a mid-level manager is likely to engage in dialogues focused on specific objectives and would find it difficult to establish relationships on par with those of a CEO. Table 2.8 outlines the typical scoring for the different levels of this parameter.

Table 2.7 Value of the Personal Network

Value	Personal Network
0	**Non-existent**; organizations that typically lack institutional relationships and do not have a dedicated PA function
1	**Under construction**; employees engage in indirect contacts through intermediaries
2	**Concentrated and limited**; one or a few individuals in the PA function have limited contacts, not necessarily at a senior level and use them infrequently
3	**Concentrated and high-quality**; one or a few individuals in the function possess key contacts and are proactive in leveraging them when needed
4	**Widespread and high-level**; a significant number of PA personnel have developed high-level contacts and consistently leverage them as needed
5	**Widespread, systematized, and high-level**; a significant number of function members possess and share high-level contacts that can be activated for business objectives

Table 2.8 Value of the Top Management Network

Value	Top Management Network
0	**Non-existent**; individuals in their first role or those transitioning from other organizations or countries
1	**Insignificant**; limited contacts with second-tier representatives or in areas tangentially related to the sector or territory
2	**To be developed**; the top manager is actively building the network, starting with a few solid contacts and leveraging their experience
3	**Structured but narrow**; direct contacts with key figures and a focused network of stakeholders
4	**Vertical, structured, and long-lasting**; long-established, mutually trusted relationships with policymakers and sector stakeholders
5	**Broad, structured, and long-lasting**; long-term, mutually trusted relationships with the majority of policymakers and key stakeholders

2.5.4   Relevance of the Company (to Institutions)

The more significant the company, the more likely policymakers are to engage with its representatives. The company's relevance is assessed based on the degree of interest institutions show toward it. Size is a key factor,

Table 2.9 Relevance of the Company (to Institutions)

Value	Relevance of the Company
0	**Not relevant or Not applicable**; typically refers to a company with no relationships with institutions
1	**Indirect relevance**; the company lacks direct relationships with institutions, but its activities influence entities that engage with public administration, either directly or through intermediaries
2	**Potentially relevant**; the company may hold relevance for institutions, but certain areas of concern remain at a potential level
3	**Group-level relevance**; the company is part of a group that holds significance for Government, but on its own, it lacks the critical mass needed to achieve a position of relevance
4	**Significant relevance**; the company operates in markets of significant interest for the development and implementation of public policies
5	**Absolute relevance**; the company plays a pivotal role in one or more areas of public interest

as it generally reflects substantial involvement in the economy and society. A large company not only generates employment but also contributes to the country's competitiveness through its business activities. The standard classification for this parameter is provided in Table 2.9.

2.5.5 Thematic Relevance

This parameter measures the importance policymakers attribute to the specific sectoral domain in which the company operates; it is therefore not an assessment of the company itself. It is important to avoid confusing this with the company's relevance, as doing so could result in double-counting its significance, that is, conflating **Company Relevance** with **Thematic Relevance**. The value scale for thematic relevance is defined in Table 2.10.

2.5.6 Public Affairs Practices

This indicator reflects the company's willingness to invest in PA. It serves as a crucial warning signal, as low values suggest a limited capacity to manage relationships effectively. Table 2.11 presents the evaluation of PA techniques and the organizational structures in place. The topic will be analyzed at a strategic level in Section 5.2 and at an organizational level in Sections 6.1 and 6.3.

After completing the analysis of the six factors, we can represent the result on a radar chart. Figure 2.6 illustrates the cases of two different companies.

Table 2.10 Thematic Relevance

Value	Thematic Relevance
0	**Not relevant**; outside the direct scope of interest of a public entity
1	**Indirect relevance**; the theme is indirectly linked to the public sector
2	**Prospective relevance**; the theme holds potential interest for institutions, but is not currently being examined
3	**Non-priority relevance**; the theme falls within the scope of competence and interest but does not hold priority or urgency
4	**High relevance**; the theme is of significant interest to at least one institution and is currently relevant
5	**Absolute relevance**; the theme is a priority for institutions, is currently relevant, and may also be urgent

Table 2.11 Value of Public Affairs Practices

Value	Public Affairs Practices
0	**Activity not conducted in the company**; typical of companies operating in areas where direct contact with institutions is not anticipated. In such cases, discussing techniques is not relevant
1	**Personal-level activity**; institutional relationships are directly managed by the entrepreneur or managers in an informal, unstructured manner. Typically, there are no dedicated techniques employed
2	**PA activities delegated to staff**; staff members are designated to handle institutional relationships and manage the processes independently. Techniques are applied on a practical, ad hoc basis
3	**PA function is in place**; it is moderately active externally but not well integrated into business processes. Techniques are partially understood and applied
4	**Active PA function**; an active PA function that operates externally and is moderately engaged internally. Dedicated techniques are used regularly
5	**Highly structured PA function**; the function is highly active in managing institutional relationships and is fully integrated into business processes. Dedicated techniques are naturally employed

These are two entities that, while generating the same thematic interest for an institution, are characterized by two distinctly different levels of potential to develop relationships. The company identified by the solid line is marked by an institutional relationship management approach centered around the company leader, without a dedicated structure. In the case of

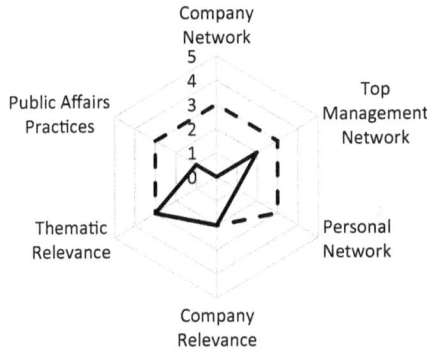

Figure 2.6 Institutional relations development potential.

Value	Company Network	Value	Company Relevance
0	Non-existent	0	Not relevant
1	Limited	1	Indirect relevance
2	Vertical	2	Group-level relevance
3	Vertical + stakeholders	3	Potentially relevant
4	Broad and active	4	Significant relevance
5	Broad, consolidated, and active	5	Absolute relevance
Value	Personal Network	Value	Thematic Relevance
0	Non-existent	0	Not relevant
1	Under construction	1	Indirect relevance
2	Concentrated and limited	2	Prospective relevance
3	Concentrated and high-quality	3	Non-priority relevance
4	Widespread and high level	4	High relevance
5	Widespread, systematized, and high level	5	Absolute relevance
Value	Top Management Network	Value	Public Affairs Practices
0	Non-existent	0	Activity not performed in the company
1	Insignificant	1	Activity performed at a personal level
2	To be developed	2	Delegated personnel
3	Structured, but limited	3	Basic PA function
4	Vertical, structured, and long-lasting	4	Externally active PA
5	Broad, structured, and long-lasting	5	Highly structured PA

the company identified by the dashed line, there is a medium level of PA structuring, with a significantly higher development potential compared to the other, and consequently, a greater likelihood of establishing effective collaborations with public entities.

2.6 Building Decision Support Reports

We introduce Decision Support Reports, analytical tools designed to track and interpret the evolution of issues across both physical and digital environments. These reports highlight the interplay between the two realms, providing valuable insights to inform strategic decision-making. Special emphasis is placed on the analysis of digital events, an emerging and innovative area in the development of PA.

We introduce a **set of factors and attributes** that must be collected and processed in order to prepare the reports.

We assign a reliability level to the collected information to ensure that heterogeneous entities are not treated in the same way. The **Reliability Classes** we will use as reference categories are as follows:

- **Certain**: regardless of the source, the information's reliability, value, and characteristics can be determined with unequivocal certainty.
- **Personal**: statements or opinions expressed by a clearly identifiable actor that may not always represent an official position of their organization. However, they can reflect an expression of intent.
- **Generic**: generally unverifiable information that often cannot be attributed to a specific entity. Despite this, it may hold relevant insights and warrant further investigation.

We identify a series of key elements that will help us define the scope of the analysis and deliver truly useful results. These elements include:

- **Politically Sensitive Objectives**: the analysis should first determine whether political actions taken during the reference period support or hinder the achievement of a specific business objective.
- **Intermediate Targets**: progress toward an objective can be monitored using a combination of indicators, including:
  - *Quantitative indicators* (e.g., percentage of target achievement).
  - *Qualitative indicators* (e.g., favorable opinions, authoritative statements on the topic).
  - *Technical indicators* (e.g., issuance of laws, regulations).

In each case, the most suitable indicator – or set of parameters – must be selected to best capture the impact of a political initiative on achieving the desired outcome.

- **Adverse Events**: two types of adverse events can occur:
  - *Predictable*: the better we anticipate potential obstacles to achieving our objective, the more effectively we can provide actionable insights to mitigate them.
  - *Unpredictable*: no matter how skilled we are, it is nearly impossible to foresee every move made by the actors within our relational arena.

- **Attention Threshold**: defined threshold levels should be set to determine when actions or statements are considered insignificant or of limited relevance.
- **Political Result Indicator**: to assess the effectiveness or risk of observed activities during the monitoring period, a result indicator should be introduced. This indicator measures the impact of identified political events on the trajectory toward the objective.
- **Observation Period**: the duration of the observation period depends primarily on the industry and the nature of the initiative being undertaken.
- **Key Actors**: identifying the most relevant institutions, intermediaries, and influencers is crucial to aligning efforts with the objectives being pursued.

In addition to these elements, it is essential to consider and **correlate processes from both traditional media communication and the WSM sphere.** These processes include:

- **WSM Listening**: the detection process consists of two main components. The first is traditional media analysis, including press reviews segmented by target audience and linked to video news from television channels. The second involves monitoring online conversations, identifying key terms and hashtags, and analyzing top influencers. In essence, all standard social media marketing tools typically used for analyzing social networks and related platforms will be employed.
- **Opinion Mining/Sentiment Analysis**: sentiment analysis focuses on identifying the overall emotional tone (positive, negative, or neutral) of a text. In contrast, opinion mining goes beyond sentiment, extracting detailed opinions on specific aspects or entities. Both are valuable tools for interpreting a DPA phenomenon.
- **Analysis and Information Extraction**: this step follows the opinion mining process and extends into the realm of prediction, which involves forecasting future behaviors and creating scenarios. At this stage, we enrich the previous steps with existing information (about the company, context, institutions, etc.) and extract insights that can inform decision-making.

To carry out the described activities, it is customary to rely on traditional digital systems (such as social media monitoring platforms, data analysis tools, etc.), which, however, will progressively be replaced by AI. AI is capable of delivering better results both in terms of systematization and focus within the scope of analysis, ultimately providing significant support for prediction activities.

In the following paragraphs, we will examine the most important reports to be developed for monitoring and managing the execution of a PA initiative.

2.6.1   Key Facts Report

First and foremost, we introduce an indicator designed to monitor the impact of political events on business objectives. This indicator will primarily take a graphical form, comparing two mathematical functions:

- **Objective Function:** to achieve a PA objective, we define a series of steps. Some of these steps may have an on/off outcome, while others may show a percentage of completion. Furthermore, some of these steps will depend solely on our activities, while others will rely on actions or decisions made by institutions or other stakeholders. This process follows a timeline determined by both company decisions and those of external actors. Given the numerous variables involved, we can create a time-bound checklist to track progress. Simultaneously, we can anticipate potential adverse events and, using the same methodology (though with greater temporal uncertainty), build a similar checklist. These checklists represent successes or failures that can be shown in a positive/negative histogram. For a more sophisticated analysis, we can merge these two sets into one and represent it as a continuous function, without attempting to interpolate data or derive an analytical expression.
- **Result Indicator Function:** while the objective function represents the theoretical plan (the forecast), the result indicator function visualizes the actual unfolding of favorable and adverse events during the observation period. These events may result from company actions, actions by other key stakeholders, or independent initiatives from institutions. Similar to the objective function, we will observe "piles" of events as they unfold. In this case, the sequence of events can also be represented as a continuous function. The recommendation is to use a simple numerical methodology or, alternatively, rely on qualitative representations that, while informed by certain data, avoid overly complex analytical calculations for visualization. It is crucial to remember that the goal is to compare the objective curve with the result indicator curve.

Note on graphical representations
The terms continuous function, interpolate data, and analytical expression are used here in a qualitative and illustrative sense. They describe graphical representations designed to visualize trends and patterns over time, not precise mathematical models or calculations. The aim is to support strategic

reflection and decision-making rather than to perform rigorous mathematical analysis.

In theory, if the two curves were to align perfectly, it would indicate a flawless PA campaign, one that achieved its objectives with maximum effectiveness and efficiency. However, in practice, this is unlikely to occur. First, because to achieve the desired outcome, we typically implement a series of redundant actions, anticipating that some of them will fail. Moreover, for high-stakes projects, it is unrealistic to expect the absence of adverse technical or political positions. These will inevitably emerge, causing fluctuations in the result indicator curve.

The dual-function graph that follows (see Figure 2.7) is designed to provide **a quick overview of whether the institutional activities required to achieve a desired result are aligning with expectations.** Using this methodology, we can observe that the objective function effectively defines two regions: one above the curve and one below it, each with the following significance:

- **Confidence Area:** when the result indicator curve lies above the objective curve, we are in the confidence area, signaling a good situation at the specific moment of observation. Being in this area indicates a favorable position, though it does not guarantee success. While we may have achieved some quick wins or incremental gains, we may not yet have reached the concrete results that define true success.
- **Risk Area:** the region below the objective curve indicates a position of difficulty or delay relative to the ideal path. This may result from unsuccessful company actions, adverse initiatives independently undertaken by institutions or third parties, or delays in expected events. The greater the distance between the result curve and the objective function, the

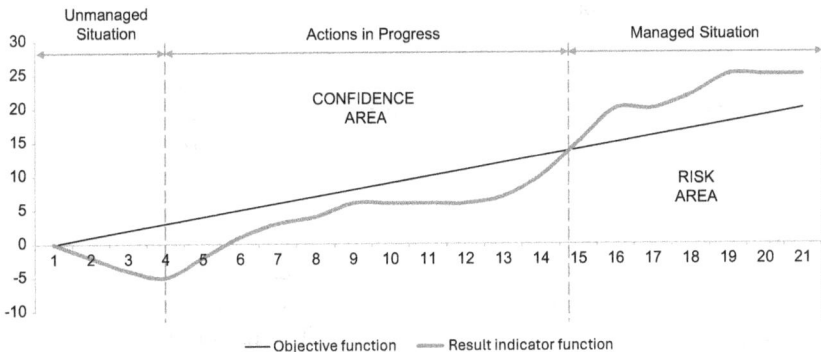

Figure 2.7 Objective function and result indicator function.

more significant the challenges. The situation is particularly concerning if a divergent trend emerges, showing that outcomes are drifting further from the desired goal. In such cases, it is critical to take corrective action, whether by strengthening PA activities, reassessing the chosen approach, or deciding to continue the initiative while accepting the risk of an unfavorable institutional position.

Figure 2.7 illustrates an example of the trend of the two curves (Objective and Result) over the monitoring period of an initiative, from its inception to its conclusion (in this case, the 21st week). Assuming the report is conducted on a weekly basis, the two curves will naturally fluctuate every seven days.

The *Result Indicator* curve clearly exhibits a nonlinear trend, influenced by the occurrence of various events – more or less significant – that cause minor fluctuations, resulting in bends in the graph. In the example shown in Figure 2.7, both the objective function and the result indicator begin at the origin of the axes, indicating a politically neutral position at the start of the observation period. At the **initial phase**, we may encounter one of the following **conditions:**

- **Favorable:** this situation arises when there are political conditions that support the initiative we are about to launch. The higher the degree of positive expectation, the higher the result indicator curve will start above the origin.
- **Neutral:** this occurs when there is no clear political position or a neutral attitude is observed, suggesting that no strong support or opposition exists.
- **Adverse:** from a graphical perspective, this refers to the area below the x-axis. In this case, we begin with the prior knowledge that there are political positions opposing the development of the initiative we are about to undertake.

Referring back to the example in Figure 2.7, it is clear that the situation progressively worsens over the first four periods. The causes of this decline could stem from immediate reactions by institutions to the launch and initial steps of the initiative or the occurrence of adverse contextual factors. Analyzing the result indicator curve, we observe a concerning downward trend in the **Risk Area** up to week 4, reaching a low point that reflects the sequence of adverse events in the preceding periods. As time progresses, positive events begin to emerge in week 5, reversing the curve's trajectory. Although the curve remains in the risk area, it gradually moves closer to the objective function. From week 15 onward, the situation improves significantly, and we enter the **Confidence Area**. By this stage, we have achieved important intermediate goals, and we have taken additional steps to solidify political support for the ongoing initiative. By week 21, the project's anticipated closing week, we see that not only have we met the expected milestone, but we have also implemented further relational actions that may prove valuable for future developments.

Creating such a plan, naturally with time horizons appropriate to the duration of the PA objective to be achieved – typically ranging from one to nine months – allows for the **determination of KPIs to measure the effectiveness of the PA function itself.** Naturally, the system is not intended for actions that need to be carried out within minutes or hours.

Let's continue using the case presented in Figure 2.7 to explore the different types of situations that may arise.

It is important to note that, in some instances, the company's objective can still be achieved despite an adverse political situation, meaning the result indicator curve may fall outside the *Confidence Area*. The political factor should be considered alongside other variables that influence the progress of the initiative.

In practice, we should treat institutional positioning as a productive factor, while making the necessary distinctions. This represents **a significant shift in defining the role of institutional relations, as they evolve into an integral component of the production process,** taking on a new position within the value chain and organizational structure.

Let's now examine the phases, keeping in mind that, in addition to the three shown in Figure 2.7, there is a fourth phase – the **Relative Risk** – that is not depicted in the example.

- **Unmanaged Situation:** this refers to both scenarios where, despite all relational efforts, adverse political developments continue to arise, and cases where no intervention is made, resulting in decisions that are unfavorable to us. From a graphical perspective, the unmanaged situation occurs when the result indicator curve is in the *Risk Area* and follows a downward trend.
- **Actions in Progress:** this phase involves taking steps to address and improve a critical situation. While we may observe both favorable and unfavorable political developments, the overall trend of the result indicator curve is upward, though it remains within the *Risk Area*.
- **Managed Situation:** in this phase, institutional manifestations are predominantly positive, and while there may be some negative signals, they remain manageable. The result indicator curve shows an upward trend and remains within the *Confidence Area*.
- **Relative Risk:** although we are still in the *Confidence Area*, the Result indicator curve begins to trend downward. This can occur due to adverse actions that threaten the achieved position or a decline in PA efforts,

often driven by the assumption that we are in a secure position. This trend is particularly risky when it appears far from the achievement of the objective, signaling that a series of adverse actions is gaining momentum and must be addressed.

The example assumes that intermediate milestones are successfully achieved. However, in practice, it may happen that **one or more milestones become unachievable** during the observation period. This situation would imply the inability to reach the final objective, necessitating the formulation of a new strategy and subsequent adjustments to the *Objective* curve and the overall planning of relational interventions. The political events we track can be either reversible or irreversible, depending on the relevant time frame for achieving the objective. When we refer to a progressive balance, we are considering both positive and negative events, not in the sense that one negates the other, but as a reflection of the prevailing or non-comparable value.

Let's distinguish between **two Types of Political Events** relevant to the observation period:

- **Substantial events:** these mainly include intermediate objectives (such as laws, administrative acts, etc.) that, once achieved, are unlikely to be questioned in the short term or within the expected duration of the activities.
- **Secondary events:** these include related events or early signals of official acts that will manifest later. This category encompasses statements, posts, interviews, etc.

All of these events should be tracked both in the weekly event chart and in the cumulative progressive chart. Alternatively, one could present only the curve representing the accumulated information, complementing it with a list of relevant events throughout the observation period. In Table 2.12, the most common traceability cases are categorized based on *Reliability* classes (*Certain, Personal, Generic*) and *Intensity* (*High, Medium, Low*), reflecting their relative relevance within each class.

As a complement to the analysis of *Key Facts*, it is always good practice to include a list of qualitatively significant acts and events that underpin the representations in Figure 2.6. These should be characterized with the attributes outlined in Table 2.12 and, if necessary, accompanied by a **brief political interpretation of the events.** This interpretation should result from organizing the observed elements and analyzing them within the context of the current political and sectoral environment. Personal opinions should be avoided, and the representation of the phenomenon should remain objective and clear.

Table 2.12 Acts and Events of Political Significance

		Reliability		
		Certain	*Personal*	*Generic*
INTENSITY	**High**	Laws; Regulations; Decisions of Authorities/ Agencies; Ordinances; Judgments	Public statements made by policymakers of all kinds involved in the matter	Non-public agreements, responses to hearings or inquiries from government representatives, and similar events
	Medium	Norms or similar acts that require subsequent implementation or are subject to further decisions; measures taken by other countries on the same matter	Public statements made by political figures in lower-ranking positions	Expressions of intent in an electoral program; framework agreements or memoranda of understanding
	Low	Outcomes of discussions in committees, councils, etc., without formal resolutions	Structured personal opinions; statements made in informal or non-public settings	Responses to spontaneous questions; information relayed on behalf of third parties

2.6.2 Behavioral Report

Now, let's analyze a report dedicated to assessing the behavior of *Key Actors*. It identifies and evaluates the main factors that characterize their actions, helping us understand their actual role in relation to the subject under consideration.

The evaluation framework relies on both qualitative and quantitative data, allowing the analyst to select the most appropriate metrics based on their expertise. The **key factors to consider** are:

- **Presence**: assesses the extent of the actor's actions in relation to the objective being monitored.
- **Coherence**: measures the actor's ability to maintain a consistent line of thought and action, even in evolving circumstances.

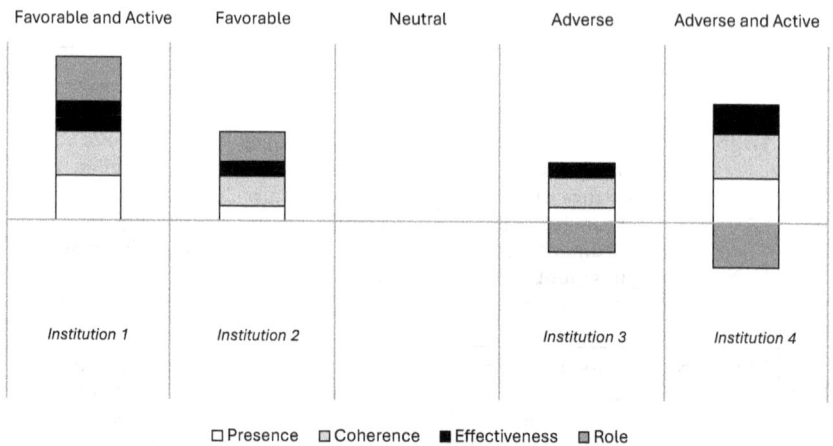

Figure 2.8 Behavioral report summary chart.

- **Effectiveness:** evaluates the actor's capacity to exert a meaningful impact on the issue at hand. Effectiveness should be assessed holistically rather than on a short-term basis. It should be measured by examining the planned trajectory, the achievement of intermediate milestones, and the actor's tangible commitment to the subject.
- **Role:** determines whether the actor's stance aligns with or opposes our position.

By assessing the various factors for each relevant actor over the reference period, it is possible to identify **recurring behavioral profiles**, as illustrated in Figure 2.8. Some actors may not only share our position but also exhibit strong activism, while others may oppose us with varying degrees of pro-activity. Understanding these **behavioral patterns** is particularly valuable, as it helps identify consistent elements relevant to the objective. The analysis generally refers to a person holding a relevant institutional position or belonging to a governing body, but the institution/intermediary could also be considered as an entity.

In the *Behavioral Report Summary Chart* example shown in Figure 2.8, we have outlined the profiles of four key actors relevant to the PA project we are working on. To create the chart, we must first establish a metric that allows us to measure the intensity of the analytical factors (*Presence, Coherence, Effectiveness,* and *Role*). This metric can also be a purely qualitative assessment, as long as it enables a meaningful comparison between the actors. Let's analyze them in detail:

- *Institution 1*: this represents the best possible "ally," a highly engaged actor on the issue, consistent (and therefore presumably reliable), fairly effective, and holding a significant role.
- *Institution 2*: this actor also shares positions aligned with ours, but at first glance, it appears to have a lower capacity to influence outcomes. All the variables observed in Institution 1 are present and positive, but with lower intensity.
- *Institution 3*: classified as an opponent, this actor holds positions contrary to ours (represented by a gray rectangle below the horizontal axis). It has low presence and effectiveness but shows a fair degree of coherence, suggesting that shifting its position may be challenging.
- *Institution 4*: a strongly adversarial actor, active and undoubtedly the leading promoter of a stance opposing ours.

This report can also be effectively applied to intermediaries. Naturally, intermediaries should be compared among themselves rather than with institutions. Ideally, comparisons should be made within homogeneous categories (e.g., experts, associations).

2.6.3 Sentiment Overview Report

This report compares actions recorded in the physical world with those in the virtual world. For completeness, we emphasize that WSM goals in the context of DPA can be divided into two categories:

1. **Simple Interpretation:** these are activities that can be measured directly using social listening tools, allowing us to assess the success of the initiative.
2. **Evaluation:** these activities cannot be evaluated using social media metrics alone, as their purpose goes beyond communication and is related to traditional actions and the company's overall objective.

The effectiveness of *Simple Interpretation* actions can be evaluated empirically by observing both the *Result Indicator Function* (see Figure 2.7) and a *new function called WSM*. Figure 2.9 presents these functions together, highlighting the presence of institutional activities (see Table 2.12 for political acts and events).

The case under consideration is highly favorable, as tangible actions prove effective, leading to a reversal in the *Results Indicator Function* during periods 3–5. Simultaneously, the WSM activities performed align with moments of success, primarily observed in intervals 3–5 and 13–15, as indicated by the arrows in Figure 2.9.

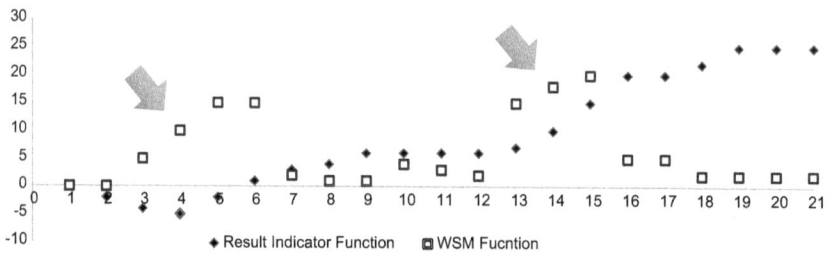

Figure 2.9 Side-by-side view of traditional and WSM actions.

The *WSM Function* representation in Figure 2.9 is constructed using a function of the form:

$$y = f(r, n)$$

where y represents the intensity of actions in a given period, determined by their relevance (r) and quantity (n). The advantage of this methodology is that it allows us to trace a trendline that illustrates the progress of initiatives relative to their outcomes. To simplify monitoring, one can report the number of WSM activities within the period, potentially adjusted according to a parameter that measures their impact.

As mentioned, the use of digital tools is essential to track and update these reports. AI will help us better understand an actor's role on a specific issue by drawing from our analyses and contextual data.

2.6.4 *Company, Opposing Stakeholders, and Context Actions*

Let's now consider a complete visualization of the analyses conducted so far, in which we integrate the actions of our competitors (in terms of PA) and all the context actors.

Let's now consider the example case (as shown in Figure 2.9) and focus on the actions taken by third parties. This helps us become familiar with our *Opposing Stakeholders* (if present) and other relevant actors. We classify this group as the *Context*. In Figure 2.10, we present the actions taken during the reference period by our *Company* (WSM), our *Opposing Stakeholders*, and the actors in the *Context*. Once again, we use a graph to show intensity, measured by the frequency and relevance of WSM actions.

It's important to remember that **digital confrontation** is not an end in itself; it **has real-world implications** or reflects tensions unfolding in the physical realm. We must be extremely careful not to make statements or take actions in the virtual space that could result in failures in the real world.

◆ Context Actions □ WSM Actions ▲ Opposing Stakeholders Actions

Figure 2.10 Company, opposing stakeholders, and context actions.

The actions carried out by the *Opposing Stakeholders*, shown in Figure 2.10, are represented by black triangles with a negative sign. It can be observed that in the first two periods, there are significant hostile WSM actions (-20 and -25 on a hypothetical intensity scale where -30 is the maximum). These actions also provoke adverse reactions from context actors directed toward us. Notably, the WSM actions contribute to the manifestation of negative real-world events in the early periods.

From period 4 onward, significant PA actions are observed, and the corresponding white squares gradually increase in value. This trend parallels the achievement of initial real milestones, which lead to a reversal of the *Results Indicator Function*, as shown in Figures 2.7 and 2.9. In the subsequent periods, initiatives of varying intensities – both adverse and favorable – emerge from the *Context*. However, the desired outcome is still within reach.

All the reports we have examined can be developed and updated either individually or together, depending on specific needs or periodic updates. They are flexible analytical tools that should always be consulted when defining a strategy or PA action plan.

Box 2.1 provides a simple tool for assessing the effectiveness of combining traditional and digital actions.

Box 2.1   Assessing the Coherence and Effectiveness of Traditional and Digital Actions

With WSM actions, we aim to contribute to the occurrence of one of the phenomena listed in Table 2.12 (*Acts and Events of Political Significance*), which may result from both traditional and digital activities. The objective from a DPA perspective is to understand whether we are effectively using WSM initiatives as a complement to

Table 2.13 Synergy between Traditional and Digital Actions

		WSM Actions	
		Success	*Failure*
TRADITIONAL Actions	**Effective**	Perfect synergy	Useless or incorrect WSM actions
	Ineffective	Incorrect WSM design	Inconsistent traditional and digital strategy or unfeasible objective

a traditional PA campaign. Table 2.13 connects traditional and digital actions.

If the field actions are effective and WSM metrics show success, we achieve perfect synergy. However, in the case of ineffectiveness or failure, we are likely facing significant errors in the strategic planning of the intervention, likely affecting both traditional and digital aspects. This scenario also includes instances where the objective is unrealistic or difficult to achieve due to constraints such as limited time, insufficient resources, or other factors.

Next, consider the situation where we achieve traditional success, but WSM metrics indicate failure. This scenario is typically linked to the ineffectiveness of online actions or their inadequate implementation. **It's crucial to understand that utilizing DPA is not mandatory; it should only be embraced when it adds value.** Inappropriate use can lead to problems that wouldn't arise otherwise. We must be cautious of digital trends that irresponsibly push the use of social media without considering its strategic fit. In the latter case, WSM metrics indicate success, but the tangible outcome is adverse. This may point to errors in designing the digital tool or in interpreting events during the observation period, which in turn led to incorrect conclusions and misguided actions.

Bibliography

Austin L.L., *Social Media and Crisis Communication*, Routledge, New York, 2018.

Bonato A., *Dots and Lines: Hidden Networks in Social Media, AI, and Nature*, Johns Hopkins University Press, Baltimore (Maryland), 2025.

Cattaneo A., Zanetto P., *Fare Lobby. Manuale di Public Affairs*, Etas, Milano (Italy), 2007.

Di Giacomo G., *Digital Public Affairs & Advocacy: From Traditional Lobbying to Blended Public Affairs*, Franco Angeli Editore, Milan, Italy, 2021.

Goidel K., Cook C., *Political Polling in the Digital Age: The Challenge of Measuring and Understanding Public Opinion*, Louisiana State University Press, Louisiana, 2011.

Harris P., Fleisher C.S., *Handbook of Public Affairs*, SAGE, Thousand Oaks, California, 2005.

Knaflic C.N., *Storytelling with Data: A Data Visualization Guide for Business Professionals*, Wiley, Hoboken (New Jersey), 2015.

Nieto A. *Harvard Business Review Project Management Handbook: How to Launch, Lead, and Sponsor Successful Projects*, Harvard Business Review, Boston, Massachusetts, 2021.

Thomson S., *Public Affairs in Practice: A Practical Guide to Lobbying*, KoganPage, London (UK), 2007.

Timmermans A., *Research Handbook on Public Affairs. Connecting evidence and Strategy*, Edward Elgar Publishing Limited, London, 2024.

Winter H., *The Business Analysis Handbook: Techniques to Deliver Better Business Outcomes*, KoganPage, London (UK), 2023.

Chapter 3

Operational Tools

3.1 Enhancing Investments

Referring to Figure 1.2 (*The Five Basic Processes of Public Affairs*), let's start by analyzing the *Enhancing Investments* process. In this case, the company has set a production goal and we are called to act as PA because either the technical effectiveness in achieving it can be improved through an institutional initiative, or there are institutional reasons that hinder its attainment. By "production," we refer to any type of activity carried out by an entity (company or association), not necessarily of an industrial nature.

The main issues we face as PA in this case are:

- **Regulatory Constraints:** the existence or absence of a regulation that prevents us from maximizing production efficiency.
- **Lack of Resources:** inadequate allocation of resources – whether financial or material – poses a significant and frequent challenge to the success of a technical proposal.
- **Resistance to Change:** this refers primarily to an explicit refusal to accept changes and innovations that disrupt established processes.
- **Excessive Bureaucracy:** administrative procedures can sometimes create a significant obstacle to the efficient development of a technical solution.
- **Information Deficiency** (regarding the solution): rejection or opposition may stem from insufficient understanding of the solution itself, rather than unawareness of its potential effects.
- **Low Priority:** the topic, and consequently our proposal, is not a priority for the institution in question.
- **Lack of Trust in the Proponent:** doubts or skepticism about the credibility of the proponent or the proposal itself can hinder its acceptance.
- **Political or Organizational Issues of the Public Entity:** internal political dynamics or organizational challenges within the public entity that may obstruct decision-making or implementation.

DOI: 10.4324/9781003647829-4

Let us now examine the **technical PA tools that allow intervention** on the issues presented. At the end of the paragraph, Table 3.4 will correlate problems and tools.

Figure 3.1 illustrates a simplified process for using PA tools to support a technical proposal to an institution. The process begins with a scouting and awareness-raising phase, followed by a technical presentation of the issue. These initial steps can be handled by a technical function without PA involvement. However, **if the issue takes on an institutional dimension, PA steps in, deploying the most suitable tools to address it.** The outcomes of these actions will naturally vary, leading to more or less favorable developments. This approach can be part of a structured PA strategy or a response to an urgent or unforeseen need, whether flagged by another corporate function or triggered by external factors, such as new regulations or technological innovations.

It can be observed in Figure 3.1 that the rectangles corresponding to the different tools are colored differently, according to a scale ranging from the highest frequency or effectiveness of tool usage in relation to *the Enhancing Investments* process, to the lowest. *Black* represents the **highest value,** Gray an intermediate one, and finally White indicates the lowest. It therefore emerges that the most frequently employed tools in this context are *Regulation Issuance* and *Agreements*, whereas *Direct Impacts* appear to be

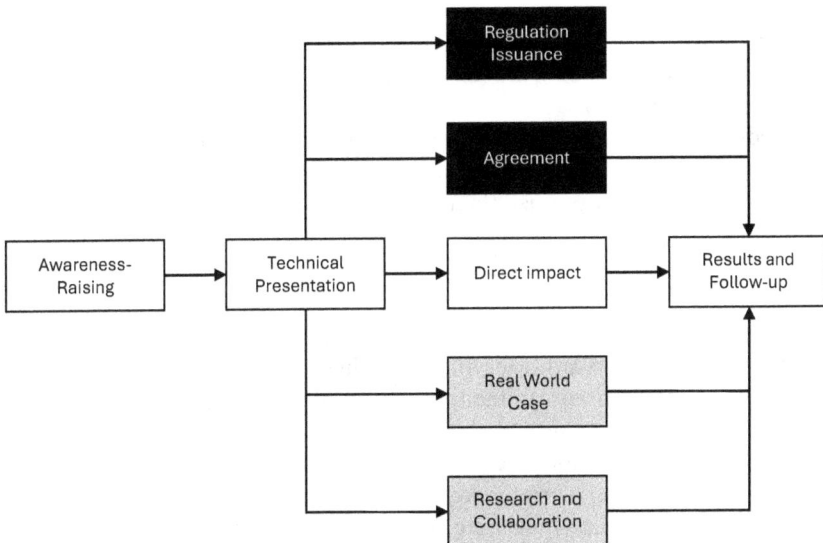

Figure 3.1 Public affairs tools to *enhancing investments*.

the least suitable for the intended purpose. Naturally, this remains a purely statistical observation; in fact, even tools that seem to be less commonly used for this objective can sometimes prove to be effective.

3.1.1 Regulation Issuance

Promoting the creation of a new regulation or the modification of an existing one to enable our company to operate more effectively is perhaps the most well-known activity in PA: **lobbying**. In this context, however, we are not referring to all lobbying efforts that might support a general position. Rather, we are focusing on **targeted actions aimed at resolving a specific issue**, such as pursuing for the adoption of a new law or regulation, pushing for the amendment or repeal of an existing provision, or working to safeguard an existing law from unwanted changes.

In practice, within Public Affairs Management, influencing the creation of regulations – lobbying – is just one of the tools in the manager's toolkit.

The use of AI in relation to this specific activity is interesting:

- **Legislative and Regulatory Data Analysis**: AI can analyze large volumes of legislative and regulatory data to identify trends, gaps, or potential changes that could benefit a particular interest. Advanced algorithms can scan thousands of legal documents, providing insights on potential law amendments or emerging regulations.
- **Legislative Drafting**: AI tools can help streamline the drafting process, identify inconsistencies, and ensure that proposed legislation aligns with legal frameworks.
- **Predictive Analytics**: AI-driven predictive tools can forecast the likelihood of success for proposed legislative changes by analyzing factors such as lobbyists optimize their strategies.

3.1.2 Agreements

Agreements are effective and widely used instruments for achieving common goals between institutions and individuals. Signing an agreement with operational implications can facilitate the implementation of an activity, as it gives concrete expression to the political will to proceed, promotes continuity in implementation, is communicable, and can be invoked in appropriate forums to assert a right. Agreements often allow for exceptions to a regulatory provision, as they are based on a mutual understanding between the parties. This enables them to achieve the same outcome, possibly on a temporary basis, while circumventing the complexity of amending existing laws.

They can take various forms and, depending on the context, may have different names: Agreement, Memorandum of Understanding, Protocol of Intent, etc.

Manifestos and Pacts also fall into this category; these are high-level instruments, sometimes unilateral, and may involve asynchronous signing. While these are tools of moral persuasion with low operational effectiveness, they are important for building consensus. However, their use is much less frequent compared to traditional agreements.

3.1.3   Direct Impacts – Benefits of a Solution

Clear and concise description of the advantages and impacts generated by an initiative (project, solution, etc.) is among the most important factors in promoting its utility to an institution. It is essential to invest adequate effort in gathering and analyzing elements that demonstrate the benefits derived from a proposal and to effectively present them. Both steps require specific skills, and PA plays a crucial role in highlighting these aspects to the public interlocutor.

The types of benefits commonly referenced to promote the validity of a solution are listed in Table 3.1, which can help identify the **key aspects of a proposal that hold value** for the institution.

With this understanding, we can act at the WSM level (and therefore within DPA, as discussed in Chapter 4, "Digital Tools") while simultaneously crafting targeted content that reinforces this aspect in meetings with

Table 3.1 Direct Institutional Benefits of a Proposal

Impact Typology	Determinants	Primary Aspects	Secondary Aspects
Technical			
	Project		
Economic			
	Return on investment		
	Efficiency		
Organizational			
	Processes		
	Responsibility		
	Organizational structure		
	Knowledge and Skill		

(Continued)

Table 3.1 (Continued)

Impact Typology	Determinants	Primary Aspects	Secondary Aspects
Communicational			
	Political		
		Quality of service	
		Tax relief	
		New service provision	
		Civil infrastructure	
		Resolution of critical issues	
		Social	
	Image		
		Performance excellence	
		Recognition	
		Innovation	
			Reference sector
			Technology used
			Technique employed
			Territorial scale
			Used products
			Implemented processes
			Existing organization
		Internationality	
		Values	
Social			
	Inclusion and Integration		
	Employment		
	Safety		
		Physical	
		Logical	
	Service Quality		

policymakers and other stakeholders identified in the Institutional Relationship Map (see Figure 2.3).

Success ultimately depends on the strategic combination of tools, relationships, content, and timing.

In this category of tools, we also include the institutional **Company Profile**, which is a true presentation of the company we represent, built by emphasizing the aspects of interest for a government entity: the company's role, size, employees, shareholders/ownership, products, investments, organization, clients, strategic projects, industry and territorial impacts, social responsibility and sustainability, code of ethics, use of AI, presence and position in the international context, and financial and stock market profile (if listed). Strictly speaking, a summarized extract of this document should be included in any occasion when engaging with public stakeholders with whom we do not have an existing relationship.

3.1.4   Real World Case

Presenting positive results achieved in a similar case to the one we are proposing strengthens the credibility of the proposal. However, this can sometimes be challenging due to the difficulty of identifying truly comparable situations. Best practices are often cited, but these are not always genuinely compatible with, or replicable in, our specific context.

The key distinction is between using our own case or a third-party case to support our thesis. While an internal case may seem more effective, it risks being self-referential and subject to criticism, as the context and parameters could appear tailored to our argument. Third-party cases, though potentially more credible, can raise concerns about replicability due to different operational contexts. However, both approaches have advantages:

a) An **internal case** showcases expertise and adaptability.
b) A **third-party case** gains credibility if conducted by a trusted entity.

Verbal exposition, even when supported by digital tools, is sometimes insufficient to fully convey the perception of a project to be realized. The immersive nature of a real experience cannot be replicated through tools that do not engage all the senses, especially for innovative or unprecedented creations.

In many cases, having a **physical object** that concretely demonstrates the concept can be highly effective. The most common scenarios where a physical demonstrator proves useful include: the innovativeness of a solution, its complexity, promotional needs, commercial investment in a client, and technical validation.

3.1.5   Research and Collaboration

The potential offered by scientific research in the field of PA is vast and highly effective. A key example is the **use of results from a scientific study** conducted by a reputable university or similar institution to support a thesis, which is a powerful tool in the PA context. However, it is crucial that the research is carried out by a neutral and respected institution to lend full credibility to the findings.

Another significant strength of this approach is the ability to conduct joint field analyses, which allow for a shared evaluation of a proposal's effectiveness. This also facilitates the creation of **discussion platforms** that promote close collaboration with institutions, addressing issues that require joint exploration and resolution. The presentation or publication of the results obtained is equally important, as it acknowledges the success of the activity carried out.

Table 3.2 outlines the main areas of application for research tools and their objectives, thus providing useful guidance for making the most appropriate intervention choice.

Table 3.2 Research and Collaboration Tools

Activities	Purposes
Technological insights	
	Demonstrating the validity of one's technological choices
	Benefiting from knowledge in sectors different from one's own field
	Demonstrating evidence of a technology's diffusion and adoption
	Providing forecasts on the evolution and development of a technology
Economic, political, and social studies	
	Analyzing macro-level impacts
	Designing economic scenarios
	Forecasting behavioral trends
Conducting field research	
	Receiving feedback on the impacts of a solution from its recipients
	Collecting feedback to improve or address issues
	Demonstrating the effectiveness of a solution
	Predicting user behaviors

(Continued)

Table 3.2 (Continued)

Activities	Purposes
Establishing joint development table	
	Building long-term strategic pathways
	Activating public-private collaborations
	Sharing diverse positions and negotiating
	Anticipating and managing critical issues
Public events for presenting research findings	
	Giving visibility to a concrete result
	Raising awareness of a topic among the target audience
	Demonstrating the company's commitment to the local community
Joint research publications	
	Highlighting the strength of a company's position
	Increasing visibility and building trust

Table 3.3 Public Affairs Technical Tools

Regulation Issuance	Agreement	Direct Impact	Real World Case	Research and Collaboration
New law	Bilateral Agreement	Technical	Proprietary case	Technological
New regulation	Convention	Economic	Third-party case	Economic
Amendment	Memorandum of Understanding	Organizational	Prototype	On-field
Suppression of law	Pact	Communication	Installation	Working Table
Protection of law	Manifesto	Social	Implementation pathway	Technical Workshop
		Company Profile	Digital simulator	Publications

In this paragraph, starting from the *Investment Enhancement* process, we have analyzed the main technical PA tools that can be deployed to achieve the result. In Table 3.3, we present them briefly to facilitate their visualization and potential selection.

At the beginning of the paragraph, we analyzed the main causes underlying the need for a PA intervention aimed at enhancing investments. In Table 3.4, we **correlate these challenges with the appropriate technical PA**

Table 3.4 Use of Public Affairs Technical Tools to *Enhance Investment*

Technical Issues	PA Technical Tools	Complexity	Condition for the Result
Regulatory constraints	Regulation issuance, Agreement	VARIABLE	It mainly depends on the provision to be promoted, and therefore on the strength of the technical justification
Lack of resources	Regulation issuance, Agreement	HIGH	Opportunity to align the initiative with other sustainable efforts
Low priority	Direct Impact	HIGH	Limited involvement of the public entity in the activities, or potential opportunities to build synergies on other topics
Excessive bureaucracy	Regulation issuance, Agreement	MEDIUM	Problem shared across several companies
Resistance to change	Research and Collaboration, Direct Impact, Real world case	MEDIUM	Sufficient time available to effectively implement change
Lack of trust in the proponent	Research and Collaboration, Real world case	MEDIUM	Tangible evidence to support the company's presentation or repositioning
Political/ organizational issues of the public entity	Research and Collaboration, Agreement	LOW	Clarity on the approach to be taken with new stakeholders
Information deficiency	Direct Impact, Real World Case	LOW	Availability of clear, precise, and well-organized information

tools to address them, indicating the average complexity of the intervention and the conditions typically required for its successful outcome.

3.2   Fostering Business Development

We now turn our attention to the set of institutional activities designed to foster a business-friendly environment. While PA does not constitute a commercial activity in itself, it plays a crucial supportive role in navigating relationships with public institutions, relying on specialized tools and strategies. In this context as well, PA initiatives are expected to produce concrete outcomes that are naturally aligned with the company's strategic objectives.

A clear and impactful example of such an initiative is the **facilitation of market entry for a product** through the introduction of targeted regulation. This regulatory framework might, for instance, encourage the adoption of technological innovation in products, the implementation of new safety standards, or the definition of specific quality requirements within a given process.

Let's begin by examining the key reasons for PA intervention in commercial matters:

- **Complex Commercial Issues:** PA activities can contribute to identifying broader solutions and removing barriers that hinder product dissemination or market entry, as well as facilitating the negotiation of complex engagements involving multiple institutional stakeholders.
- **Innovativeness of the Proposal:** an innovative and even brilliant proposal may not be understood or adequately contextualized, may not be compatible with current regulations, or may need to overcome the tendency to purchase established products.
- **Joint Projects:** the opportunity to engage in joint projects or simply respond to tenders issued by third parties in collaboration with a government entity often necessitates the creation of institutional consensus and the development of robust partnerships with multiple stakeholders.
- **Company Presentation:** an effective presentation to institutions is undoubtedly the first crucial step in building future business relationships.
- **Inadequate Demand:** for a public entity, identifying a need does not automatically mean being able to adequately represent it.
- **Difficulty in Identifying an Interlocutor:** when there is no single point of contact for an issue, institutional intervention is often useful.
- **Need for Change:** this refers to the necessity of bringing attention to institutions regarding inadequate management practices or administrative procedures, not tied to a specific product or public entity, but rather to cross-cutting issues that affect multiple stakeholders.

As will be evident, some cases are similar to those addressed in the *Enhancing Investments* process. Similarly to what we did in that case (see Table 3.4), Table 3.5 identifies the most suitable PA technical tools (see Table 3.3) to address the typical issues in the *Fostering Business Development* process.

For *Difficulty in identifying a counterpart*, no technical PA tools have been identified; in fact, only relational tools – which will be analyzed in the following paragraphs – can be used for this purpose (see Table 3.6).

Table 3.5 Use of Public Affairs Technical Tools to *Foster Business Development*

Commercial Issues	PA Technical Tools	Complexity	Condition for the Result
Complex commercial issues	Agreement, Regulation issuance	HIGH	Will from the interlocutor to identify a resolutive path
Innovativeness of the proposal	Direct impact, Real world Case, Research, and Collaboration, Regulation issuance, Agreement	HIGH	Tendency of the public entity to introduce incremental or radical innovations, managing their benefits and impacts
Need for change	Direct impact, Real world Case, Research and Collaboration	HIGH	The issue at hand must be common to multiple stakeholders and supported by intermediaries as well
Inadequate demand	Real world Case, Research and Collaboration	MEDIUM	Willingness on the part of the public entity to be supported in identifying the need and analyzing existing market solutions
Difficulty in identifying a counterpart	–	MEDIUM	Deep knowledge of the subject in question and its professional network
Joint projects	Agreement, Research and Collaboration	LOW	The company we represent is recognized for its competence and reliability in the environment where it operates
Company presentation	Direct impact	LOW	The company must present a compelling profile to the institutional interlocutor

Table 3.6 Public Affairs Relationship Tools

Meeting Formats	Communication Formats	Discussion Formats
Quick chat	Quick message	One-on-one interaction
Networking meeting	Speech	Small group discussion
Scheduled meeting	Slides deck	Working group session
Event	In-depth analysis	Public debate

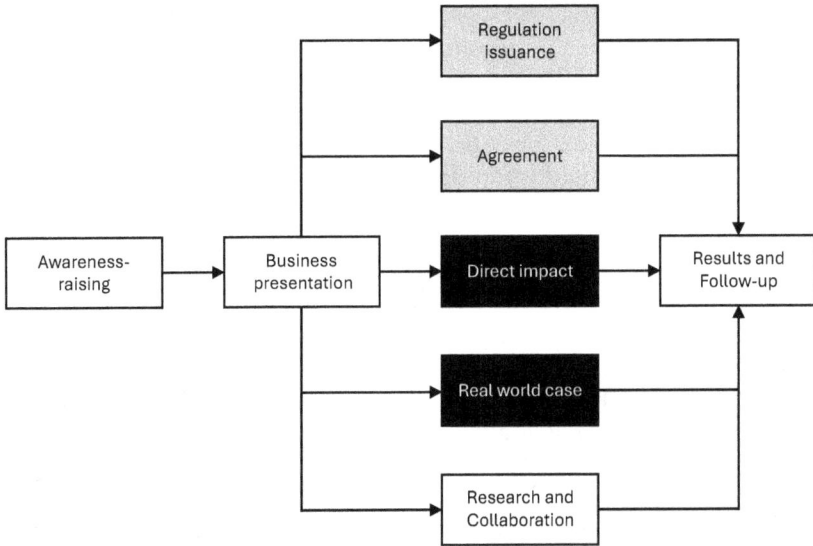

Figure 3.2 Public affairs tools to *foster business development.*

Also in this case, a typical *Fostering Business Development* process can be outlined, largely aligned with the one presented in Figure 3.1, except that the *Technical Presentation* step is naturally replaced by the *Business Presentation.* As previously discussed, if the activity carried out by the relevant function (such as Marketing or Sales) does not lead to a successful outcome, appropriate PA initiatives will be activated.

Observing the PA tools shown in Figure 3.2, it is clear that their frequency and effectiveness in the *Fostering Business Development* process differ from what is observed in *Investment Enhancement.* In this case, *Direct Impact* and *Real World Case* are the most frequently used to convey our position to the public counterpart, while *Regulation Issuance* and *Agreements* are employed only secondarily. Finally, *Research and Collaboration* rank lowest in terms of application.

3.3 Establishing and Developing Institutional Relationships

The initiation of a relationship is logically the first step in its development. This phase is extremely delicate and requires experience, as a misstep could jeopardize the future relationship, complicating the management of subsequent stages.

The choice of approach and how the relationship should be built vary significantly depending on both the **time frame** within which we anticipate needing to engage concretely with that stakeholder and the **objective** we aim to achieve. Figure 3.3 illustrates the process flow to be implemented based on these two factors (time frame and objective).

In Figure 3.3, we start from the assumption that the individual we intend to meet holds a position we consider relevant to our objectives within the *Institutional Relationship Map* we have drawn (see Figure 2.3), and that we have thoroughly analyzed this actor by collecting information from various channels, thus developing an *Institutional Stakeholder Profile* (see Figure 2.1). As shown, the two activities are connected by a double-headed arrow, as their development process is iterative: the more important the actor under examination is deemed to be, the more in-depth and developed the *Institutional Stakeholder Profile* becomes.

The first step to be carried out will be to get to know our counterpart in order to initiate the relationship. After that, we will have the following options:

- **Objective: Defined – Timing: Immediate.** We know exactly the result to be achieved and we are in a position to immediately launch an institutional action and therefore proceed with one of the previously analyzed processes (*Enhancing Investments, Fostering Business Development*).
- **Objective: Defined – Timing: Deferred.** The goal is known, but the time is not yet right to start either of the two targeted processes, for whatever reason (waiting for other relevant events to occur, needing to structure the relationship with the counterpart, consolidating activities and the role of other stakeholders, etc.). It is therefore necessary to enter a *Relationship Development* process aimed at strengthening the relationship and beginning to work on those content-related aspects that lay the groundwork for achieving the objectives we will soon begin working on.
- **Objective: To be refined – Timing: Deferred.** We are in a situation where timing is not yet ripe, and the objective itself also requires further refinement in order to begin working toward it. As in the previous case, we must initiate a *Relationship Development* process, and once both the objective and timing are clearly defined, we can implement initiatives for *Enhancing Investments* or *Fostering Business Development*.
- **(Objective: To be defined – Timing: Immediate).** This option is not represented because it does not reflect real-world scenarios.
- **Objective: Undefined – Timing: Undefined.** This activity corresponds to the **classic network-building process**. It is based on the assumption that we may need to collaborate with certain actors, but we do not yet know when or for what purpose. This kind of need often arises suddenly and requires urgent attention, this is the typical **firefighting lobbying activity**, which cannot be part of a structured, planned effort. Since neither the objective nor the timing has been defined, it makes no sense to initiate a *Relationship Development* process.

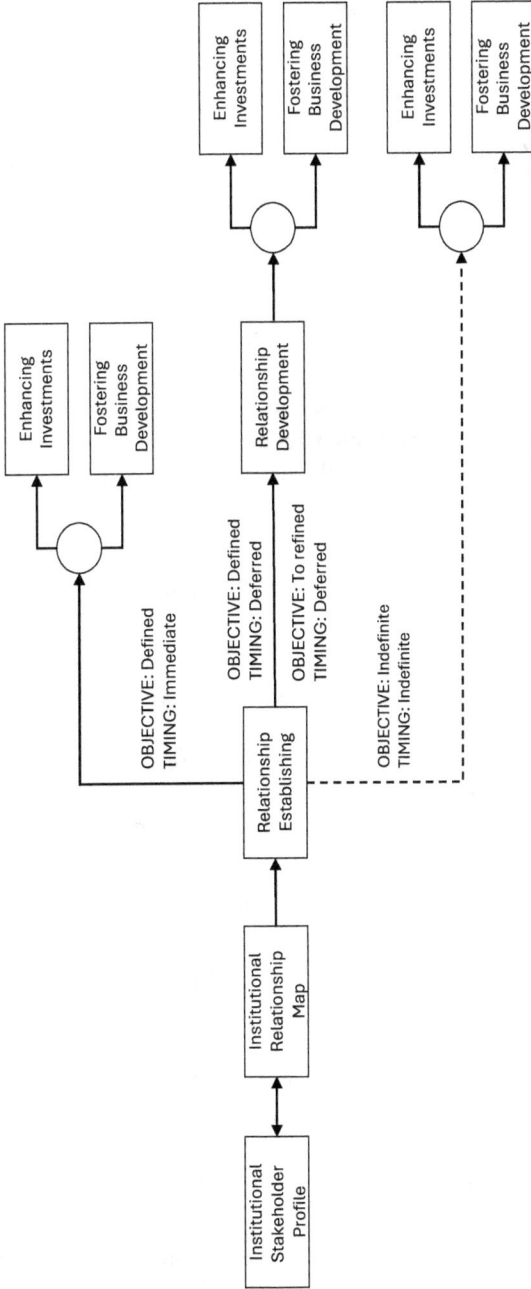

Figure 3.3 Flow of public affairs processes.

As shown in Figure 3.3, **any Public Affairs activity always concludes with either an** *Enhancing Investments* **or a** *Fostering Business Development* **process**. If this is not the case, it means we have simply wasted time and resources.

Once the *Institutional Stakeholder Profile* has been completed and the engagement scenario has been clarified, the next step is to **identify the most appropriate form of contact**. For this purpose, we introduce the *Public Affairs Relationship Tools* (see Table 3.6). Many of these tools are relatively intuitive; therefore, we provide a concise description below:

- **Meeting formats**: the principal typologies of engagement settings:
  - *Quick chat*: a brief and informal exchange.
  - *Networking meeting*: any occasion specifically designed to foster interactions among multiple participants.
  - *Scheduled meeting*: a formally arranged and structured meeting.
  - *Event*: any public or closed-door event in which a speech or formal intervention may take place.

- **Communication formats**: the various modalities through which a message can be conveyed:
  - *Quick message*: a minimal and essential piece of content.
  - *Speech*: a structured message delivered to an audience, regardless of its nature or size.
  - *Slide deck*: a presentation composed of organized and thematically structured content.
  - *In-depth analysis*: a document or presentation containing technically detailed and extensively developed content.

- **Discussion formats**: the different configurations in which stakeholders may interact:
  - *One-on-one interaction*: the traditional bilateral exchange.
  - *Small group discussion*: typically involving a limited number of participants.
  - *Working group session*: any form of closed-door dialogue, potentially involving a large and heterogeneous set of participants, including those previously unknown to one another.
  - *Public debate*: a confrontation or exchange of views conducted in a public forum.

All of these formats can be implemented either in person or virtually, with the exception of the networking meeting. **The decision to conduct these interactions in a physical or digital setting also constitutes a key design element of the PA strategy.**

For a very first contact, you can take advantage of either a *networking meeting* or a *quick chat*, maybe on the sidelines of another event. But when it comes to starting a connection that you hope will turn into some form of collaboration, a *scheduled meeting* is always the best way to start off on the right foot.

Box 3.1   Lifecycle of the Institutional Relationship: Time to Be Invested in Relationship Development

We have seen that, in some cases, it is necessary to invest in developing a relationship with a stakeholder in anticipation of future collaboration, typically in the short to medium term. In this section, we examine the typical **stages in the life cycle of an institutional relationship,** explore the different levels of trust required for an effective partnership, and outline the most effective methods for relationship development. This activity, however, cannot be open-ended; it must eventually lead to tangible opportunities within a reasonable time frame. A **time horizon of three to nine months** is generally appropriate.

A natural question emerges: **how much time should we reasonably invest in developing a relationship** with a stakeholder?

To answer that, let us consider a scenario in which we have identified and analyzed the appropriate stakeholder, but we do not yet know what specific contribution they might make to a given issue or when the relationship is likely to become relevant.

To estimate how much time to invest, let's analyze the phases in the life cycle of the relationship:

- **Subject Analysis and Intervention Planning**
  This phase begins immediately after identifying the subject. The analysis should be concise, ideally lasting one to two weeks. If it requires additional field research, a few extra days may be necessary. In any case, this stage should remain brief, ranging from a single day up to one month in particularly complex situations.
- **Intensive Development**
  This is the core phase, where all efforts focus on building and strengthening the relationship in the field. Its duration depends on the strategy in place, which may define specific windows of opportunity for action. While this phase can range from one to six months, in practice, it should typically be kept within two to three months to maintain momentum and clarity.
- **Consolidation**
  At this stage, progress has been made, but either a concrete collaboration opportunity has yet to emerge or the timing isn't right

to act on it. This phase can last anywhere from three to six months, but extending it much further risks diluting the momentum and weakening the relationship.

- **Activation**
  This is when the groundwork pays off, and the relationship transitions into concrete technical or commercial collaboration. At this point, the dynamic shifts from development to execution.
- **Cooling-Off**
  Gradual disengagement occurs here, without formally ending the relationship. This may happen due to:

  a) Failure to establish a meaningful connection.
  b) The subject not playing the expected role in our strategic context.
  c) External changes undermining the original assumptions for engagement.
  d) The relationship having run its course with no further utility.
  e) An excessively long development timeline that no longer aligns with our goals.

In practice, we've broken down the *Relationship Development* process into *Intensive Development* and *Consolidation*, the **total duration of which should never exceed a calendar year.** Typically, it stays under six months.

3.3.1   Actions for Relationship Development

Let us examine the main techniques available to strengthen the relationship. It is important to note that all actions described here are functional to the achievement of our objective, even though they may not be directly linked to it. The techniques can be grouped into **three categories**, as the factors that support the development of the relationship are based on the transfer of information, the implementation of joint activities, and the execution of communication and relational initiatives.

Information Activities

a) **Promoting awareness of the topic of interest.** It is useful to identify and periodically share relevant, concise, and clear content with the institution, targeting both policymakers and their staff. This should be done primarily through digital channels – such as email or direct messaging – to ensure timely and effective communication.
b) **Sharing significant information.** Relevant developments that highlight the company's activities (e.g., economic results, investments, awards) may be communicated to institutional counterpart.

c) **Providing access to corporate expertise.** When the company has distinctive expertise, it can be shared with the institution, including through training programs or educational initiatives.

Collaborative Activities

d) **Engaging the institution in relevant activities.** It may be helpful to identify areas of corporate activity in which the stakeholder is already engaged, or to explore opportunities to involve them in one or more of these areas, even if only through our passive participation.

e) **Exploring opportunities for joint projects.** Based on the stakeholder's areas of expertise, potential projects involving some form of public-private collaboration may be identified, regardless of their nature.

f) **Offering support for institutional initiatives.** When the institution organizes public events aligned with the company's business interests, potential forms of participation should be considered, including opportunities for brand visibility.

g) **Collaborating through intermediaries involving the institution.** Take part in initiatives, such as projects, events, or working groups, promoted by intermediaries that also involve the stakeholder.

Relational and Communicational Activities

h) **Organizing meetings with corporate leadership.** Plan institutional meetings with senior executives (such as the President or CEO) to highlight the strategic importance we place on the relationship being developed.

i) **Attending the institution's events.** Taking part in public occasions where the stakeholder is present, even a brief greeting or informal exchange, can contribute to strengthening the relationship.

j) **Strengthening the relationship with policymaker staff.** Consolidate interactions with the policymaker's team by sending tailored content based on their specific knowledge and competencies and by organizing dedicated meetings to facilitate information sharing.

k) **Inviting the stakeholder to speak at corporate events.** For public events organized by the company that align with the stakeholder's expertise, it may be effective to involve them as a speaker and engage them in shaping their contribution.

It's always best to **combine multiple techniques** rather than rely on a single one. The most effective strategies are those that blend different approaches to relationship-building, creating a more robust and well-rounded engagement. For this reason, it's recommended to apply one or more techniques from each of the three categories previously outlined. This ensures that all key success factors are addressed. That said, it's important to use *Collaboration* tools with care. For example, it may not be appropriate – given our specific goals

– to activate both activity (d) and (e) at the same time. By contrast, techniques in the other two categories are generally compatible, though their use should still be thoughtfully managed.

Finally, it's essential to remember that no matter which techniques are used, we must avoid being intrusive. At this stage, the initiative we're promoting is unlikely to be a top priority – or even a pressing concern – for the stakeholder.

Box 3.2   Levels of Confidence in an Institutional Relationship

As a relationship evolves, the level of trust among the actors involved also changes. For effective institutional collaboration, **it is not necessary to achieve absolute trust**, but rather a sufficient degree that allows the relationship to function in a professional, fair, and transparent manner. Let us now examine the different levels of trust to better understand their implications and assess our current position:

- **Total trust.** A state of complete confidence, where no formal or informal obstacles hinder collaboration. Communication is open, and mutual support is taken for granted.
- **Relative trust.** A generally positive level of trust, characterized by openness to dialogue and a willingness to share information relevant to joint efforts.
- **Cordial trust.** A neutral and pragmatic stance. The relationship is neither strongly embraced nor rejected; the other party engages with transparency but maintains emotional distance.
- **Detached trust.** This attitude suggests a passive disinterest or implicit disregard for the relationship, often indicating that the company is perceived as low priority.
- **Hostile.** An openly negative posture. The relationship is actively rejected, whether due to past experiences, conflicting interests, or general incompatibility.

In the first column of Table 3.7, the defining attributes of each level of trust are outlined. These attributes can be directly observed through interactions with the subject in question. The table cells further specify and qualify the listed attributes. We can consider the **institutional relationship** to be adequately established once we identify elements that allow us to place it **at the level of *Relative* or *Cordial* trust.**

Table 3.7 Levels of Confidence in an Institutional Relationship

	1 Complete Trust	2 Relative Trust	3 Cordial Trust	4 Detached Trust	5 Hostile
Presence of a genuine, individual bond beyond formal roles	Personal connection				
Willingness to discuss confidential or delicate topics	Openness on sensitive matters				
Inclination to provide information, resources, or insights		Willingness to share			
Acknowledgment of the other party's expertise and value		Recognition of competencies			
Willingness to engage in dialogue			Readiness to maintain constructive communication		
Respect for roles			Clear understanding and appreciation of each party's position and responsibilities		
Lack of interest				Passive disconnection, with minimal effort to build or maintain the relationship	
Uncooperative attitude				Avoidance or refusal to collaborate, without open conflict	
Intolerance					Active rejection of perspectives, values, or practices; low emotional acceptance
Contempt					Open disdain or devaluation of the other party, often expressed explicitly or through behavior

3.4   Relational Risk Management

Let's delve deeper into the *Relational Risk Management* process (see Figure 1.2).

Over time, tensions or critical issues between a company and an institution are bound to arise; it's a natural aspect of any long-term relationship. These situations must be approached with clarity and foresight, **ensuring that institutional dialogue is maintained even in times of crisis.** This helps avert the escalation of the issue and safeguards the broader relationship. A mature and well-established rapport often makes it possible **to isolate specific issues, preventing them from affecting other areas of collaboration** between the company and the public entity. The strategic application of relationship-preserving techniques plays a key role in effectively managing relational risk.

AI can play a significant role in identifying potential risks. By correlating the full range of activities carried out by a company with current regulations, political guidelines, economic planning, and other contextual factors, AI is able to detect critical patterns that may not have been previously considered and that warrant further analysis.

As just mentioned, **following a corporate decision or an institutional policy, a potential point of friction may arise between a business and a public authority.** Consider, for instance, a government introducing a new sector-specific tax that directly affects the company or mandating technical upgrades that lead to increased operational costs. The issue may also originate from the company itself, such as when it decides not to invest in a technology identified as strategic by a public body or chooses not to operate in a territory designated as a priority by the Government.

Regardless of whether the origin of the issue lies with the public actor, the company itself, or a third party, the business must approach the situation with awareness and strategic intent. In this context, the role of the PA manager becomes crucial. It is their responsibility **to closely monitor both institutional developments and internal corporate decisions,** and to alert senior leadership when a potential misalignment with public authorities is emerging. A comprehensive analysis must follow, aimed at gathering all relevant information to **assess the full impact of the decisions at hand,** in terms of possible tension or conflict with public institutions.

Typically, two scenarios may unfold:

1. *A decision made by a public authority* adversely affects the company or the company deems it inappropriate to comply with the directive received.
2. *A business initiative goes against the guidance provided by the public authority* or the authority has rejected a proposal submitted by the company.

In such circumstances, the **company generally faces three strategic alternatives:**

- **Accept the directive.** This course of action may be chosen when the company assesses that the impact of the measure is limited, or that the risks associated with non-compliance outweigh those of compliance. Acceptance may involve shelving a planned initiative or refraining from initiating legal proceedings against a regulation deemed improper. In essence, this option avoids open conflict and preserves the institutional relationship.
- **Pursue a negotiation.** This strategy involves a willingness to make concessions in exchange for reciprocal flexibility from the counterpart, with the aim of reaching a mutually sustainable solution. If successful, negotiation can defuse the issue while partially safeguarding the company's original objectives. However, if the resulting compromise skews too heavily toward one party's interest, the situation may revert to a binary choice between compliance and opposition.
- **Oppose the directive.** While always acting within the boundaries of the law, a company is not necessarily obliged to follow recommendations issued by public authorities. Although compliance is generally advisable, there are cases in which a request – to act or refrain from acting – may be considered unsustainable or misaligned with corporate goals. **Choosing not to comply may indeed provoke institutional tension.** This is the clearest scenario in which relational risk management becomes essential, with the goal of preserving long-term relationships, whatever their nature. beyond the immediate issue at hand.

Having defined the possible scenarios we may encounter, we will now examine the *Critical Issue Assessment*. We will therefore introduce the *Relational Risk Profile Sheet* as an operational tool for managing relational risk, and finally, we will outline the main risk *Mitigation Actions*.

3.4.1   Critical Issue Assessment

We now move into the operational phase by introducing the following parameters, which allow us to assess the impact of a critical issue on the institutional relationship. The **qualifying elements of the critical issue** we consider are:

- *Origin.*
- *Intensity.*
- *Timing of occurrence.*
- *Maturity of the relationship.*

We have just examined the **Origin**, which refers to whether the issue arose from an action taken by the company followed by a reaction from the institution or vice versa. In some cases, the root cause of the issue may also originate from a third party.

Next, we consider the **Intensity** of the critical issue in institutional relationships. This refers to the severity of a potential situation, assessed by the consequences it may generate if and when it materializes.

To assess the *Intensity* we propose a straightforward **three-level scale: high, medium, and low,** based on two key parameters:

- **The importance of the public counterpart,** assessed through an analysis of the public entity's relevance in relation to our organization. For didactic purposes, we will limit ourselves to introducing two categories of institutional counterparts: those with higher relevance, referred to as *Primary*, and those with lesser relevance, defined as *Secondary*. The criterion for distinguishing between these two classes should be based on a factor that allows for effective classification of public actors, for instance, their *Institutional, Technical*, or *Business relevance* (see Table 2.1), evaluated qualitatively; the expected contribution in terms of *business* or *economic efficiency*, assessed quantitatively (see Section 5.1); the *importance of the relationship* (γ, analyzed in Section 5.1) or another parameter, possibly a combination of the above.
- **The impact of the issue on the relationship.** From a relational standpoint, the emergence of a critical issue can produce two main outcomes:
  - *Cooling down*: a gradual deterioration of the relationship that does not lead to its termination but significantly undermines its overall quality and the intensity of engagement.
  - *Termination*: a complete breakdown of the relationship, which may be temporary or permanent, sudden or planned, and either mutually agreed upon or unilaterally imposed.

By combining the *importance of the public counterpart* with the *impact of the issue on the relationship*, it becomes possible to classify the *Intensity* of the critical issue, as illustrated in Table 3.8.

Table 3.8 Critical Issue Intensity in Institutional Relationships

Critical Issue Intensity	Importance of Public Counterpart	Effect on the Relationship
High	Primary	Termination of a relationship
Medium	Primary	Cooling down of a relationship
	Secondary	Termination of a relationship
Low	Secondary	Cooling down of a relationship

Table 3.9 Assessment of a Critical Issue

Origin	Intensity	Timing	Relationship Maturity
Company Initiative	High	Past	Non-existent
Institutional Measure	Medium	Imminent	In Development
Third-Party Action	Low	Short-term	Mature
		Long-term	

Naturally, the model for determining the *Intensity* can also be developed in a more sophisticated manner, for example, by categorizing counterparts into clusters based on their level of importance or by introducing more specific variables to classify the impacts.

Now we introduce the **Timing of Occurrence**. We distinguish the following cases:

- **Past**: we can precisely define the moment in the past when it occurred.
- **Imminent**: expected to occur within a few hours to a few days.
- **Short-term**: expected within a month from the current date.
- **Medium/long-term**: expected to manifest in six months or later.

The final attribute to consider is **Maturity of the Relationship**. This is relevant because the impact of a critical issue on the institutional relationship is greater the weaker the relationship is, particularly in terms of its resilience. The possible values this attribute can take correspond to the typical stages in the life cycle of a relationship:

- *Non-existent.*
- *In Development.*
- *Mature.*
- *In Decline.*

Table 3.9 displays the qualifying attributes of a critical issue and the corresponding values they can assume.

Further components essential to the development of the *Relational Risk Profile Sheet* are outlined below.

3.4.2   *Register of Past Critical Issues*

We need to establish a *Register of Past Critical Issues* containing summarized information on how each issue emerged and was subsequently resolved. The register should only include significant events from the past five years. There is no predefined minimum or maximum number of entries;

Table 3.10 Register of Past Critical Issues

Timing	Intensity	Nature	Importance of the Counterpart	Summary	Effects	Historical Relational Risk (ρ_{pi})
Recent (from xxx to yyy)	High	Institutional	Primary	...	...	3
Distant (2y)	Medium	Technical	Secondary	...	...	2
Remote (5y)	Low		Secondary	...	...	1

however, it is essential that those included accurately reflect the historical state of the relationship.

The register should include the following fields:

- **Timing:** the period during which the critical issue arose and was resolved.
- **Intensity:** classified as *High, Medium,* or *Low* (see Table 3.9).
- **Nature:** indicate whether the issue was *institutional, technical,* or *commercial*. This distinction is particularly important.
- **Importance of the Public Counterpart:** classified as *Primary* or *Secondary* (see Table 3.9).
- **Summary:** a brief description of the issue and how it was resolved.
- **Effects:** a summary of the relational consequences resulting from the issue.
- **Historical Relational Risk (ρ_p):** this indicator reflects the quality of the relationship over recent years. A low value indicates the absence of relational issues, while the maximum value of 3 signals a highly conflictual relationship with the entity. A specific value (ρ_{pi}) should be assigned to each critical issue (each entry in the table), and the overall (ρ_p) is obtained by calculating the average of these values.

Table 3.10 provides an example of such a register.

3.4.3   Register of Open Critical Issues

We now shift our focus to open issues. As we did for past cases, we define a set of attributes to help qualify and categorize them. In this instance, we introduce a number of new parameters that reflect the specific dynamics of the current situation. Below, we present these parameters in detail, refer-ring the reader to the previous section for those already discussed:

- **Timing:** the date on which the issue is considered to have emerged, along with any forecast for its resolution, if available.
- **Description:** a concise description of the ongoing issue.
- **Complexity:** the degree of difficulty posed by the issue, categorized as *high, medium,* or *low.*
- **Relationship Maturity:** the current stage of the relationship life cycle, as defined in Table 3.9.
- **Risk Mitigation Activities:** the actions being undertaken to address the issue, specifically from a relational risk management perspective.
- **Stakeholder Stance:** the attitude of the institution toward resolving the issue, classified as *proactive, neutral,* or *obstructive.*
- **Current Relational Risk** (ρ_n): for each entry, based on the available evidence, we assess the level of relational risk (ρ_{ni}), defined as the prob-ability of negative impacts on institutional relationships. Using the stan-dard scale from 0 to 3, we calculate the overall risk score (ρ_n) as the average across relevant cases.

An example of the register is provided in Table 3.11.

3.4.4 *Register of Future Critical Issues*

When projecting into the future, the level of uncertainty in our estimations reaches its peak. In such a context, a solid understanding of the past and present becomes essential for building credible and meaningful forecasts. As previously discussed, AI can play a crucial role in supporting this pro-cess, helping to identify plausible scenarios by integrating internal analyses with forecasts of contextual and governmental developments.

To construct these forecasts, we begin with the current state of institu-tional relations. This is assessed by algebraically summing the average val-ues attributed to the synthesized evaluations of past and ongoing issues. The result is a numerical value ranging from 0 to 6, offering a preliminary indication of the level of attention that should be allocated to a given issue.

Drawing on the *Register of Past Critical Issues* (see Table 3.10) and the *Register of Open Critical Issues* (see Table 3.11), it becomes possible to identify particularly sensitive areas, that is, domains in which criticalities have occurred more frequently. The narrower the scope of analysis, the easier it becomes to direct strategic attention and resources. If no predomi-nant area of concern emerges, then all future initiatives planned by the company that might affect institutional stakeholders should be monitored with equal diligence.

Table 3.11 Register of Open Critical Issues

Timing	Description	Intensity	Nature	Complexity	Relationship Maturity	Risk Mitigation Activities	Actual Relational Risk (ρ_{ni})
From ...	...	Medium	Technical	High	Mature	...	2
Today	...	To be defined	Institutional	To be defined	Mature	To be defined	NA
From ...	...	Medium	Institutional	Medium	In development	...	3

As was done for past and current issues, a dedicated list of variables is defined to guide the analysis and projection of future criticalities. These new analytical dimensions include:

- **Timing**: the anticipated time frame in which the issue may materialize: *short-, medium-,* or *long-term.*
- **Origin**: the primary source of the issue: the *company* itself, an *institution* or a *third party.*
- **Intensity**: in this case, it refers to the forecast of intensity.
- **Probability of occurrence**: a qualitative estimate generally classified as high, medium, or low.
- **Risk Mitigation Activities**: any actions that are planned or already underway to reduce the likelihood or impact of relational risks.
- **Future Relational Risk** (ρ_f): for each prospective initiative identified as potentially problematic, a specific risk indicator (ρ_{fi}) is assigned. This reflects the weighted likelihood of a relational issue arising, based on the aforementioned factors. The usual risk scoring method is applied (scale 0–3).

An example of the completed register is presented in Table 3.12.

3.4.5 Relational Risk Profile

In this section, we have defined all the elements required to construct the *Relational Risk Profile* of the institutional actor under consideration. Let us now summarize the components to be included in the corresponding profile sheet.

The first value to record is the **Risk Index**, which represents the overall relational risk level. It is calculated as the sum of risks across three temporal dimensions: past, present, and future:

$$\rho = \rho_p + \rho_n + \rho_f$$

The index ρ ranges from 0 to 9 and may include decimal values. For detailed calculation methods, refer to Tables 3.10, 3.11, and 3.12. Given that the significance of risk can vary depending on the time frame, it is useful to further qualify the numeric index with one or more letters indicating the predominant contribution: **p** for *past*, **n** for *now*, and **f** for *future*.

For example, if a subject has an overall risk score of 6 – resulting from a score of 2 in each of the three time periods – the corresponding index would be **6pnf**. If, instead, the breakdown is past = 1, present = 3, and future = 2, the index would be expressed as **6n**, indicating that the present component weighs more heavily in the overall evaluation. From a PA perspective, a **6n** warrants significantly more attention than a **6pnf**, as it reflects a more immediate risk exposure.

Table 3.12 Register of Future Critical Issues

Timing	Origin	Description	Intensity	Nature	Probability	Risk Mitigation Activities	Future Relational Risk $\left(\rho_f\right)$
Short term (1 month)	Company	...	Medium	Commercial	High	...	2
Medium term (6 months)	Institution	...	High	Technical	Medium	...	3
Long term (1 year)	Third party	...	Low	Institutional	Medium	To be defined	1

A **second** important indicator is the **Risk Benchmark**, which is particularly useful for defining intervention priorities. It provides a measure of the relative risk level across the public entities under consideration. It is expressed as the deviation of an individual risk score (ρ_i) from the simple average risk score (ρ_m).

This is calculated as: **Risk Benchmark** $= \rho_i - \rho_m$.

A positive value indicates that the subject's risk level is higher than the average, suggesting greater strategic attention may be required.

The **third** summary indicator is the **Risk Trend**. Since the risk index ρ_i evolves over time, performing periodic assessments enables us to verify whether relational risk is being managed effectively. In the profile sheet, we record the variation between the current and previous year's values $(\rho_i - \rho_{i-1})$. A positive result indicates a worsening of the subject's relational risk profile. This type of analysis can be extended to the entire institutional portfolio to monitor overall risk exposure and its fluctuations.

Following these three summary indicators, the profile should include a **concise narrative description** of the subject's risk profile. This section should highlight relevant mitigation actions currently underway, as well as anticipated developments in terms of both impact and timing.

To complete the *Relational Risk Profile* (see Figure 3.4), the sheet should include the **Risk Registers** (see Tables 3.10, 3.11, and 3.12), which provide detailed evidence supporting the summary indicators described above.

It is worth highlighting that AI proves extremely useful in this type of analysis, particularly for scenario forecasting and for identifying the mitigation actions with the highest likelihood of success.

3.4.6   *Relational Risk Mitigation Actions*

In the previous paragraphs, we introduced the concept of *Relational Risk Mitigation Actions*, designed to prevent a critical issue between an institution and a company from compromising their institutional relationship. Let us now examine these actions in greater detail:

The main initiatives for mitigating relational risk include:

- **Internal and external listening and information gathering:** PA teams should regularly collect and analyze information from all available internal and external sources to track developments that could affect the evolution of a potential crisis. This ongoing monitoring provides the foundation for planning effective mitigation actions. The most relevant insights should be recorded in the *Relational Risk Profile* (Figure 3.4).
- **Mitigation Plan:** this is a structured program that outlines the mitigation activities to be implemented in response to a critical issue or a potential threat. It should clearly define the actions to be taken with

Public Entity: ....

Importance: Primary/Secondary

Risk Trend (1y)	Risk Index	Risk Benchmark
$\rho_i - \rho_{i-1}$	ρ_i (p/n/f)	$\rho_i - \rho_m$

Brief overview of the relational risk situation

...

Register of Past Issues

Timing	Intensity	Nature	Importance	Summary	Effects	Historical Relational Risk (ρ_{pi})
...	...	...	...	...	...	...

Register of Open Critical Issues

Timing	Description	Intensity	Nature	Complexity	Relationship Maturity	Risk Mitigation Activities	Actual Relational Risk (ρ_{ni})
...	...	...	...	...	...	...	...

Register of Future Issues

Timing	Origin	Description	Intensity	Nature	Probability	Risk Mitigation Activities	Future Relational Risk (ρ_f)
...	...	...	...	...	...	...	...

Figure 3.4 Relational risk profile.

institutional stakeholders, including the timing and methods of engagement. The plan must remain flexible to adapt to the evolving dynamics of the crisis and should incorporate multiple scenarios, depending on the nature and severity of the relational risk.

Main actions to include in the Mitigation Plan:

1. **Transparency measures:** These involve proactively sharing relevant information related to business decisions throughout the entire crisis life cycle. Transparency is a key instrument that demands the ability to

interpret the potential impacts and evolution of a crisis. It can also be employed at the highest corporate level and often represents the first essential step in identifying a solution and maintaining institutional dialogue, even during a crisis.

2. **Collaborative risk intelligence:** When both parties share a genuine willingness to cooperate, all possible technical and strategic avenues for managing the crisis are explored jointly. This results in a continuous, solution-oriented brainstorming process that not only seeks to resolve the issue but also helps preserve the spirit of collaboration.

3. **Strengthening unrelated collaborations:** A crisis should be contained and prevented from contaminating other areas of existing cooperation with public stakeholders. When feasible, efforts should be made to reinforce ongoing collaborations unrelated to the crisis, ideally by launching new initiatives or extending the duration of existing ones. This helps safeguard long-term institutional relations from being affected by the specific issue at hand.

4. **Institutional Advocacy:** Advocacy remains a powerful tool, even in times of crisis. Reaching government stakeholders indirectly through respected and credible intermediaries – those who are likely to be listened to – can significantly support relational risk management. It can also serve to bridge the gap between opposing positions that may have triggered the crisis.

5. **Escalation:** At the appropriate moment, involving top corporate leadership can prove to be an effective way of opening a direct channel of communication with political decision-makers, particularly when an administrative or technical resolution no longer appears viable.

In Table 3.13, we illustrate how each of these tools should be deployed, depending on the phase of the crisis: before, during, or after its occurrence.

Table 3.13 Relational Risk Mitigation Actions

Actions	Pre-crisis (Preventive)	During the Crisis	Post-crisis
Internal and External Listening	Early identification and assessment of potential critical issues	Understanding the parties' intentions and ongoing developments, including contextual factors	Gathering signals of issue resolution and identifying new areas for development

(Continued)

Table 3.13 (Continued)

Actions	Pre-crisis (Preventive)	During the Crisis	Post-crisis
Mitigation Plan	Includes regular review meetings, report updates, and focus on high-risk areas	Becomes a full-fledged action plan aimed at keeping institutional dialogue open	Revision of the plan based on the crisis experience, stakeholders involved, and most effective tools
Transparency Measures	Sharing general information and updates related to joint activities	Sharing more confidential and scenario-based information	Return to pre-crisis information sharing, with increased frequency and openness
Collaborative Risk Intelligence	Based on technical analysis of potential risk areas, including AI-based insights	Continuous multi-level brainstorming with high frequency and new content to address	Maintain the dedicated working group until completion, then return to pre-crisis collaboration methods
Institutional Advocacy	No additional actions beyond existing advocacy initiatives	Use of established advocacy channels to convey key messages for relational risk management	Continue delivering messages to reinforce the end of the crisis until advocacy efforts conclude
Escalation	Regular management of institutional relations. Initiation of a basic relationship as a minimum requirement	Organization of high-level meetings, possibly frequent and using diverse formats	Scheduling of regular follow-up meetings

3.5   Achieve the Perfect Advocacy Project

The concept of advocacy we refer to is the one described in Section 1.1. Unlike PA, which involves ongoing relationship management with institutions, advocacy is designed as a project with a clear goal, a set of specific actions, and a defined time frame. In this sense, an advocacy campaign acts as a targeted intervention that supports a broader PA strategy when a particular issue or objective requires focused, short-term engagement.

To plan an advocacy project effectively, it's essential to understand the context in which you operate: the policy landscape, the key institutional players, and the organization's position. Although the content and tactics may vary from one sector to another, many advocacy tools are flexible and can be applied successfully in different settings.

This section introduces a toolkit of practical and widely used advocacy actions. Some of these tools may also be used by opposing actors; however, we intentionally leave out any that conflict with professional ethics. One notable example is the use of fake news, a harmful and unacceptable practice that should be firmly condemned. Unfortunately, it can sometimes appear in advocacy campaigns, and it is crucial to recognize it for what it is, something we should never, under any circumstances, adopt ourselves.

Table 3.14 presents the **main advocacy tools**, imagining their application within a *perfect advocacy project*, one that leverages all available options in a coordinated and strategic way. In practice, however, even the most sophisticated campaigns should focus on a **carefully selected set of actions**, those most aligned with the specific objective, the context, and the likelihood of generating meaningful impact. In Table 3.14:

- the **Traditional Approach** column describes in-person or offline activities.
- the **Digital Approach** column outlines online tools and communication channels.
- the **Target Audience** column identifies the primary recipients or beneficiaries of each action.
- the **AI Applications** column, where relevant, highlights how AI can support or enhance the execution of specific tasks.

These actions typically unfold over the course of several months. Depending on the evolving context and interim results, they may be carried out sequentially or in parallel. Strategies can be adjusted as needed along the way.

Table 3.14 Actions of a Perfect Advocacy Project

Advocacy Action	Traditional Approach	Digital Approach	Target Audience	AI Applications
Engagement of qualified Think Tanks	Studies, focus groups, and seminars	Webinars and recorded clips	All stakeholders	Data analysis, policy forecasting, and message optimization
Development and activation of a dedicated website	= =	Web as a native technology	All stakeholders	SEO (Search Engine Optimization), traffic analysis
Definition and dissemination of a scientific thesis supporting the position	Scientific research and publication	Prevalent diffusion on the WSM with targeted messaging for user segments	General public	Assisted writing, content summarization
Recruitment of authoritative testimonials	Meetings and negotiations	WSM to communicate the presence of testimonials	Intermediaries (research organizations) and then everyone	Influencer analysis, reputation scoring
Publication of a manifesto presenting the theses	Ideation, drafting, printing	WSM for dissemination	General public	Engagement tracking
Building an effective narrative	Ideation and in-person dissemination	Widespread and targeted dissemination through the WSM	Primarily individuals, then some intermediaries, and finally others	Audience sentiment analysis, narrative testing
Activation of dedicated social media sessions	= =	Social media sessions to amplify initiatives	General public	Engagement analytics

(Creation and dissemination of "fake" news)	*Ideation and drafting*	*Legacy for data analysis, web, and social media for dissemination*	*Primarily individuals, then some intermediaries, and then others*	*Detection of disinformation patterns*
Expansion of the supporters' network	Meetings with stakeholders sensitive to the proposal	Chat for contact management, followed by WSM dissemination	General public	Network analysis and community detection
Institutional meetings	Organizing in-person meetings	Dissemination of the results of the meetings on WSM	Intermediaries, individuals	Sentiment analysis on feedback
Activation of affiliated websites or blogs	= =	Web as a native technology	People interested in the specific topic	Traffic source monitoring
Creation of dedicated graphics	Ideation	Specialized applications	Individuals	AI-assisted design tools
Press conferences	Ideation and involvement of speakers	WSM for dissemination and potentially for consumption/usage	Institutions, intermediaries	Speech-to-text, viewer analytics
(Utilization of direct and indirect legal actions against the counterparty)	Legal proceedings	WSM media to promote/raise awareness about the actions	Institutions and businesses directly	Legal precedent analysis, risk forecasting
Identification or establishment of competence centers to support the thesis	Organization of the center and meetings	Dissemination of the center's activities through WSM	General public	Knowledge base development, thematic clustering

(Continued)

Table 3.14 (Continued)

Advocacy Action	Traditional Approach	Digital Approach	Target Audience	AI Applications
Legislative and regulatory proposals	Proposals for norms and similar acts	WSM to promote the actions and gather proposals	Institutions	Impact forecasting, stakeholder sentiment analysis
Provision of professionals for various purposes, to induce spontaneous actions of support	Aggregation of entities	WSM for dissemination; email and chat for contact	Individuals, intermediaries	Engagement prediction
Voluntary and involuntary thematic blending	Meetings, seminars	WSM and email for promotion	Primarily individuals	Topic mapping, audience clustering
Public launch event	Physical organization of the event	WSM for dissemination, email and chat for promotion	Institutions, individuals, intermediaries, businesses depending on the event	Audience segmentation, stream analytics
Crowdfunding for self-financing	Meetings, seminars	WSM, email, and chat for promotion; Open legacy for digitizing the donation process	Individuals	Fraud detection, donor behavior analysis
Media space buying	Traditional media	Advertisements on WSM, including search engines	General public	Ad performance optimization

Territorial event campaign	Physical organization of events	WSM, email, and chat for promotion	Institutions, individuals, intermediaries, businesses	Geotargeting, campaign impact analysis
Presentation of the thesis in institutional settings	Hearings, questions, committees, etc.	WSM for dissemination	Institutions	Speech analysis, semantic feedback classification
Publication and dissemination of viral videos	Conceptualization and recording of clips	Video distribution on native social media platforms and WSM	Individuals	Virality prediction
Launching petitions on general or specific aspects of the thesis	In-person signature collection	Signature collection through dedicated social media platforms (e.g., Change.org), promoted via WSM and chat channels	Individuals	Signature verification, user behavior modeling
International affiliations or international partnerships	Meetings for sharing	Legacy for analysis; WSM for dissemination; chat and email to support activities and contacts	Institutions, individuals, intermediaries	Partner mapping, engagement monitoring
Communications and written requests directed to institutions	Postal mail	WSM to amplify and disseminate the action	Institutions	Sentiment tracking, audience profiling

(Continued)

Table 3.14 (Continued)

Advocacy Action	Traditional Approach	Digital Approach	Target Audience	AI Applications
Consensus building on digital channels	= =	WSM primarily to recruit supporters of the initiative	Individuals, intermediaries	Supporter behavior prediction
Sponsoring events or initiatives related to the proposed thesis	Financial support and potential participation	WSM to amplify participation	Institutions, intermediaries	ROI analysis of sponsorship
Launching training courses for enthusiasts and supporters	Organizing classroom-based courses and training	WSM for the dissemination and delivery of e-learning courses	Individuals	Learner profiling, adaptive content
Participating in third-party events, even on other topics, to present the thesis	Negotiating participation	WSM to promote participation and communicate presence	Institutions, individuals, intermediaries	Impact analysis, participation prediction
Supporting third parties on loosely related initiatives	Meetings to offer support	WSM to communicate the support provided	Individuals	Engagement effectiveness analysis
Public demonstrations	Organization	WSM, chat, and email to engage supporters and give them visibility	Institutions, individuals	Crowd sentiment forecasting
Advocating for the thesis on online channels focused on other topics	= =	Publishing posts and comments on WSM to keep the topic alive	Individuals, intermediaries	Topic relevance monitoring

	Production and distribution of items	Utilizing the WSM for sales and free distribution	Individuals	Targeting for engagement and conversion
Merchandising			Individuals	
Building a chronology, thus creating a narrative of the journey	Documenting the moments in person and drafting the text	Gathering digital elements from the WSM and making the journey visible	Institutions, individuals, intermediaries, businesses	Timeline generation, memory activation
Organizing awards related to the topic being addressed	Ideation and presentation seminars	Communication of the initiative through WSM, email, and chat	Individuals, intermediaries	AI-curated nominations, outreach targeting
Twinning with supporters of related campaigns	Signing agreements and establishing collaborations	Sharing via WSM on dedicated online occasions	Institutions, individuals, intermediaries	Network similarity detection
Launching cultural and artistic initiatives related to the thesis	Stimulating artistic production and organizing exhibitions	Promotion of artworks via WSM	Individuals, intermediaries	Emotional analysis
Diversifying the focus topic to avoid a decrease in attention	Launching related campaigns	Repeating the main thesis journey using all digital tools	General public	Topic fatigue prediction

Bibliography

Avner M., *The Lobbying and Advocacy Handbook for Nonprofit Organizations, Second Edition: Shaping Public Policy at the State and Local Level*, Fieldstone Alliance, New York, 2013.

Cima X., *Lobbying in the Real Word. A Practical Guide to Effective Advocacy*, Year One Partners, Madrid (Spain), 2023.

Darcy N., *The Secret Art of Lobbying. The Essential Business Guide for Winning in the Political Jungle*, Biteback Publishing, Hull (United Kingdom), 2019.

Di Giacomo G., *Institutional Marketing & Public Affairs: Managing Institutional Relations to Create Value for the Business*, Franco Angeli Editore, Milan (Italy), 2019.

Frohnhoefer R.W., *Risk Assessment Framework. Successfully Navigate Uncertainty*, PPC Group, San Diego (California), 2014.

Hillson D., *The Risk Management Handbook: A Practical Guide to Managing the Multiple Dimensions of Risk*, KoganPage, New York, 2023.

Kteleh T., *The Six Pillars of Advocacy: Embrace Your Cause and Transform Lives*, Tarek Kteleh, 2021. https://www.amazon.com/Six-Pillars-Advocacy-Embrace-Transform-ebook/dp/B09KP3BK27/ref=tmm_kin_swatch_0#detailBullets_feature_div

Levine B.J., *The Art of Lobbying, Building Trust and Selling Policy*, CQ Press, Washington D.C., 2009.

Libby P., *The Lobbying Strategy Handbook. 10 Steps to Advancing any Cause Effectively*, SAGE, Thousand Oaks (California), 2012.

Luttrell R., Wallace A.A., *Public Relations and the Rise of AI*, Routledge, New York, 2025.

Nussbaumer Knafic C., *Storytelling with Data: A Data Visualization Guide for Business Professionals*, Wiley, Hoboken (New Jersey), 2015.

Potrikus T., *Lobbying 101, What is it, Exactly that You Do?* Ted Potrikus, 2023. https://www.amazon.com/Lobbying-101-What-exactly-that-ebook/dp/B0CKB7257H/ref=tmm_kin_swatch_0#detailBullets_feature_div

Chapter 4

Digital Tools

4.1 Social Media as a Lobbying Tool

The use of Social Media tools in **Digital Public Affairs is appropriate only in certain cases**. Let's look at the main ones:

- **Advocacy Projects**: these are the most important area of application for DPA. The need for a collective communication strategy in advocacy – aimed at building a critical mass sufficient to ensure effective message delivery to policymakers – maximizes the utility of social networks. **A project-based approach is the most effective way to harness this tool,** as both Advocacy and DPA inherently require a system of heterogeneous, multi-level actions that must be carefully planned and executed within a project framework. Table 3.14 shows the DPA activities best suited to each phase of an Advocacy Project.
- **Need for broad visibility**: social media channels are a natural tool for amplifying initiatives that require this type of support.
- **Reactions to online activity**: social media monitoring may detect a post relating to institutional topics, which must then be managed in line with institutional relations management guidelines.

As a general rule, DPA is most appropriate for initiatives that require public engagement or visibility. In other words, social platforms are not a one-size-fits-all solution and should not be used indiscriminately.

4.1.1 How Social Media Supports Lobbying

In today's digital age, the internet and social media have become embedded in both personal and professional life. While their general functionalities are widely understood, this chapter focuses on **how these tools can be**

DOI: 10.4324/9781003647829-5

leveraged strategically in the field of lobbying and advocacy. In particular, we explore their relevance within the framework of DPA, identifying key objectives:

- **Content Dissemination.** Social media platforms offer an unparalleled opportunity to share content strategically. In a lobbying context, each post should align with a clear communication and relational plan. *Spontaneity*, where it appears, is carefully orchestrated. The objective is precise: to reach a specific audience – whether broad or highly targeted – typically institutional actors capable of interpreting and acting on the message. Content may include announcements, policy proposals, data, or public statements and must be tailored to resonate with the intended audience. Importantly, digital messaging functions within a broader ecosystem of communication tools. There is no obligation to be exhaustive; selectivity in what is shared and when is a core strategic choice designed to maximize impact and outcomes.
- **Building Credibility and Generating Consensus.** These two goals often go hand in hand. Credibility is the foundation, built through authenticity, consistency, and the ability to provide verifiable and authoritative content. Consensus, in turn, stems from trust and alignment, fostered through repeated and coherent messaging. Social media supports this process by enabling ongoing, diversified engagement. Unlike traditional communication, the boundaries between credibility-building and consensus-building are blurred in digital contexts, especially when the target is individual stakeholders.
- **Narrative Construction and Storytelling.** Long-term advocacy projects benefit from a compelling and coherent narrative. The digital environment is ideal for shaping and reinforcing such storytelling over time. From the moment a project begins, there is a story to be told, a narrative rooted in the initial motivations and developed through milestones, activities, challenges, and results. Social media allows for this narrative to evolve dynamically, incorporating both planned content and real-time developments. When integrated with visual and multimedia tools, such as videos and infographics, storytelling becomes a powerful lever for engagement and persuasion.
- **Creating Digital Hubs: Websites, Pages, Blogs.** A robust online presence is essential for modern "lobbying." Websites, social media pages, and blogs serve not only as content repositories but also as key relational platforms. Their structure and usability are critical: a poorly designed website or outdated interface can undermine even the strongest content. Conversely, user-friendly design, interactive features, and secure access areas enhance credibility and facilitate engagement. In this category, we can also include digital-first initiatives such as webinars and live streams,

which replicate in-person formats but offer new dimensions of interactivity and scalability.

- **Expanding Support Networks.** Digital tools facilitate the expansion of supporter networks, both quantitatively and qualitatively. Online platforms enable outreach to broader audiences while also supporting targeted engagement with strategic intermediaries, such as experts, associations, or research institutions. The ability to scale networks is a key advantage of digital lobbying, but it requires tailored approaches. Mass outreach campaigns differ significantly from one-to-one engagements with high-value stakeholders and social media enables both, if used strategically.

- **Announcing Initiatives.** Social media excels at the rapid and widespread announcement of initiatives. Whether sharing information about an event, a new publication, or a campaign milestone, these platforms allow for instant and far-reaching communication. However, this visibility comes with reduced control over the narrative. Posts can be reshared, reframed, or commented on in unintended ways. These dynamics must be anticipated as part of risk management and the message must always be designed with the institutional target in mind.

- **Launching Petitions.** Petitions are a time-tested form of public engagement, and digital platforms have significantly improved their reach and credibility. Tools such as *change.org, ipetitions, avaaz.org, openpetition* have normalized online petitioning, overcoming the skepticism and logistical challenges of traditional signature collection. They provide a transparent, accessible channel for mobilizing support, particularly from individuals who hold influence or represent key constituencies. When integrated into a broader advocacy strategy, petitions can serve as both a signal of public sentiment and a lever of institutional pressure. This is the typical tool of **Grassroots Lobbying** (see Section 1.1).

4.1.2 Qualifying a Post in Digital Public Affairs

Let us examine the key attributes of a post that may be of interest from a DPA perspective, when published by third parties on any platform:

- **Author.** At times, the post is signed or clearly attributable to a specific individual. In such cases, it is easier to assess the author's institutional or professional role and to gain insight into the motivations and context behind the content. When the post is instead issued by a group or a social media team, it becomes more complex to identify the individuals involved and to interpret the post's underlying purpose.

- **Content.** The core message of the post is the primary aspect to analyze. Each word should be carefully considered; no potential lead should be ignored. It is crucial to read between the lines, grasp the full implications of the message, and attempt to infer the rationale behind its publication. Apparent inaccuracies may be intentional and should therefore be interpreted within the broader relational and contextual framework. The writing style can also provide useful clues: comparing it with other posts from the same author may help determine whether a lack of precision is deliberate or simply due to time constraints.

- **Platform.** When the post appears on a social network, the choice of platform can offer additional interpretive value. If the same content is published across multiple platforms, this may indicate a coordinated communication strategy or a broader initiative with strategic relevance.

- **Official References.** Not all digital environments allow for detailed documentation, but the presence – or conspicuous absence – of structured references can be significant. If references are expected yet omitted, this may suggest a deliberate communication choice. It is important to assess the credibility and relevance of any sources cited, distinguishing between informal mentions and formal, authoritative documents.

- **Mentioned Individuals.** The explicit mention of individuals can help reconstruct the motivations behind the post and clarify its intended message. In shorter formats, such mentions are less common, unless the person holds a particularly visible or influential role. Context remains essential: posts of this kind often refer more to political figures than to administrative personnel.

- **Date.** Timeliness is a fundamental aspect of interpretation. While posts typically refer to recent or ongoing events, it is important to consider that older news may be deliberately repurposed to fit a current narrative. Distinguishing between the publication date and the actual date of the event referenced – such as the announcement versus the signing of an agreement – is key to understanding the post's significance.

- **Multimedia Elements.** The inclusion of photos, videos, or documents adds communicative value, especially when there is a clear intent to reinforce the message visually. Conversely, if the message is more ambiguous or abstract, visuals may be absent. In some cases, images may be deliberately decontextualized to support a specific interpretation, which may not align with the actual content of the news.

- **Reactions Received.** Once a post is online, it begins to generate engagement, likes, shares, comments, and other forms of interaction. The topic itself strongly influences this response. It is essential to distinguish between general popularity and qualified reactions. A "like" from a credible source may indicate implicit endorsement, though it rarely resolves the underlying issue. Comments may provide useful insights, but expectations should be kept realistic, especially if the post is part of a carefully managed strategy. Occasionally, a partially informed user may offer a helpful observation that opens a new line of interpretation, though such cases are rare. The quantity of reactions does not in itself validate any single narrative, as engagement can be compatible with multiple – sometimes contradictory – interpretations.

- **Previous Posts on the Topic.** If the post is part of an ongoing communication series, it becomes easier to analyze: the author's or editorial team's style is already familiar, and fewer uncertainties arise. However, if the topic is addressed in this format for the first time, it is worth asking why it has been selected now and who the intended recipients of the message may be.

4.2 Launching the First Post: Opening the Institutional Dialogue Online

Let us now turn to the first post, the launch of a topic, the initial spark of an online discussion or content-sharing initiative. This moment marks the beginning of an institutional dialogue in the digital sphere. One of the key decisions at this stage is whether to publish the content directly under the company's name or to delegate the task to an external party. The latter option can be strategically valuable, depending on a variety of factors:

- **Knowledge of the Topic.** When operating in a problem-setting phase, before fully launching the topic, it can be helpful to introduce background elements that will be referenced later. In this context, having a recognized expert publish the first post can add credibility and set the tone. This choice helps lay the groundwork for future messaging, allowing subsequent content to reference authoritative contributions already in circulation.
- **Direct Relevance to the Company.** A fundamental question is whether the company – or any other actor leading the advocacy initiative – should be the visible protagonist from the outset. If so, it should directly handle the topic launch. Conversely, if a more strategic, phased approach is preferred, an authoritative third party can be tasked with introducing the issue, allowing the company to step in later without overshadowing the broader narrative.
- **Level of Collaboration.** Delegating the launch of a topic requires a solid, collaborative relationship with the chosen actor, either already established or actively being built. The involvement must be coherent with prior or ongoing joint efforts, ensuring the post aligns naturally with the shared narrative and is not perceived as dissonant or opportunistic.

- **Strategic Opportunity.** In some cases, the ideal first post may come from a figure who, while not necessarily an expert, has distinctive characteristics that make them particularly suited to the moment. This choice should be guided by the project's goals, the nature of the topic, and the desired follow-up conversation. Timing can also play a crucial role, associating a topic with a figure who is particularly relevant in a given moment can create significant initial traction.
- **Managing Challenges.** Long-term advocacy projects are likely to face criticism or diminishing engagement over time, a common risk in DPA. Overexposure and repetitive messaging can lead to audience fatigue. A simple strategy to mitigate this is to have third parties introduce topics, maintaining engagement and avoiding the perception of self-promotion. From this perspective, choosing how to handle the first post becomes a foundational step in managing one's digital presence over time.

The discussion above refers to scenarios in which the company takes the lead in crafting and publishing the first post, defining its content, approach, and timing in the first person. However, the strategy shifts significantly when the organization is instead called upon to **respond to a first post** initiated by others.

This type of reaction is not necessarily defensive or negative. On the contrary, when favorable communication originates from an institution or other relevant actor, it should be treated as a strategic opportunity. Such moments call for **swift and skillful engagement,** ensuring the message is echoed, amplified, and – when possible – incorporated into a broader narrative that makes it more accessible to diverse audiences.

Table 4.1 provides a practical guide to this process. The rows list the strategic **objectives** for using Web and Social platforms, while the columns identify the main **actors** who could publish the first post. Each cell offers recommendations on the most appropriate actor for initiating a topic, based on the specific objective.

- **Black cells** indicate the most effective configurations.
- **Gray cells** represent valid, but secondary options.
- **White cells** signal scenarios where that actor is not recommended for initiating the first post.

At a glance, the table reveals that the **company** – understood as the entity driving the advocacy effort – is consistently the most effective actor for launching a topic. Meanwhile, the objective that offers the broadest range of effective configurations is **generating credibility and consensus,** reinforcing the importance of strategies that **avoid a self-referential tone** and instead emphasize collaboration and external validation.

Table 4.1 The Most Effective Actor for Publishing the First Post

	Institutions	Intermediaries	Company	Influencer
Content Dissemination	Not recommended for general informative content; more appropriate for specific messages	Advisable when opening topics that complement or support the company's narrative	A typical and frequent activity directly managed by the company	Often effective as trailblazers to introduce or amplify content
Building Credibility and Generating Consensus	A favorable official position can serve as a strong starting point, the first post itself	An authoritative intermediary's supportive post is highly valuable	The most common, direct, and effective option – even through repurposing third-party content	Less effective for initial posts, but valuable for follow-up sharing and engagement
Narrative Construction and Storytelling	Unlikely to initiate storytelling unrelated to their own institutional scope	Can be relevant when the intermediary plays a significant role in the advocacy project	The primary actor responsible for constructing and leading the narrative	Useful for enriching ongoing narratives, especially after the topic has been introduced
Creating Digital Hubs	Rare, but possible when institutions create a digital presence on a specific topic	Suitable when launching pages closely tied to the intermediary's identity or mission	Typically the main actor in opening new digital channels with their own content	Can play a key role by starting discussions on their platforms

(Continued)

Table 4.1 (Continued)

	Institutions	Intermediaries	Company	Influencer
Expanding Support Networks	Institutional content can be reused as a first post by other actors	Rarely initiates the process; may occur in specific, context-driven cases	By definition, the company leads this task	Can play a significant role by initiating topics and drawing new attention
Announcing Initiatives	Useful in joint or coordinated initiatives	Appropriate when the initiative is owned or co-owned by the intermediary	Usually the main promoter, for both independent and collaborative initiatives	Can boost visibility and, in certain cases, even launch the initiative
Launching Petitions	Can primarily occur when the public entity represents an oppositional force to the governing institution	Relevant when the petition brings together actors from a region or sector	Primarily responsible for launching petitions that align with its position	Useful for increasing visibility, though rarely responsible for the first post unless context-specific

Let us now explore in detail the **attributes – and, more importantly, the strengths – that each category of actors listed in Table 4.1 can bring to advocacy initiatives:**

- **Representativeness.** This attribute primarily refers to associations, which act on behalf of their members and, in many cases, represent an entire sector or geographical area. Their collective voice carries weight and legitimacy in institutional dialogue. This parameter was analyzed in relation to intermediaries in Section 2.2.
- **Authority.** Authority is the recognized expertise of an actor – whether an individual or an organization – in a given field. This not only legitimizes their involvement in the discussion but also adds credibility to the advocacy effort itself.
- **Network.** A robust network includes relevant institutional, scientific, and economic contacts that can be mobilized through existing relationships. The ability to activate such connections significantly enhances the impact and reach of advocacy actions.
- **Followers.** Influential actors often have highly specific and engaged followings, which can be extremely valuable in DPA, especially when these audiences are difficult for the company to reach directly. Leveraging these communities allows for more targeted and authentic engagement.
- **Impartiality.** The perceived independence of an actor – the ability to express positions in a fair and unbiased manner – is a critical asset in advocacy. Impartiality significantly enhances the credibility of a message, especially when the actor is seen as free from direct interests in the matter. It is also important to consider whether the actor is structurally or financially linked to stakeholders with a vested interest in the topic. For example, a research organization funded by private companies may produce high-quality and objective studies, but the association with industry funding alone can be enough to raise questions about the neutrality of the findings, even when the research is conducted with complete integrity and in good faith.
- **Safeguarding.** In certain situations, it may not be strategically advisable for a company to enter into direct confrontation, particularly when political dynamics are involved. In such cases, **external actors can serve as buffers,** helping to defend the company's position and protect its reputation without exposing it directly.

4.2.1 Differentiating Posts for Public Affairs Objectives

Let us now examine how to tailor posts specifically for DPA purposes. In essence, this involves assigning distinct strategic functions to common content formats so they can effectively serve different advocacy goals.

To maximize the effectiveness of a post, it is crucial to align three core dimensions with the communication objective:

- **Content.** The message itself, what is being said. This includes tone, clarity, relevance to the advocacy goal, and consistency with institutional positioning. A post aimed at building consensus will have a different content structure than one designed to mobilize support or address a policy issue.
- **Format.** The technical and visual presentation of the post. This includes the type of media (text, image, video, infographic), length, structure (e.g., bullet points vs. narrative) and whether it is standalone or part of a thread or series.
- **Distribution.** Where and how the post is published and disseminated. This refers to the choice of platform (e.g., LinkedIn, X/Twitter, institutional blog), timing, use of hashtags, or tagging.

Each of these elements must be carefully adapted to the post's objective (e.g., informing, engaging, influencing) to ensure the message resonates with the intended audience and supports the broader advocacy strategy. Table 4.2 outlines the characteristics that each attribute must possess in relation to the specific DPA objective.

Table 4.2 Attributes to Differentiate Posts by DPA Objective

	Content	*Format*	*Distribution*
Content Dissemination	Informative; can be general or topic-specific	Simple, direct, and impactful; journalistic tone	All web and social media channels are suitable; chat services may also be used for amplification
Building Credibility and Generating consensus	Clear and assertive messages; often includes explicit requests or calls to action	Structured, authoritative, and confident in tone	Targeted dissemination, primarily on platforms such as X, LinkedIn, Telegram
Narrative Construction and Storytelling	Fact-based content enriched with interpretation and commentary	Prosaic, engaging, and immersive	Regular updates via web and social platforms; no direct push actions

(Continued)

Table 4.2 (Continued)

	Content	Format	Distribution
Creating Digital Hubs	Content with multiple levels of depth; dynamic and adaptable to diverse audiences	Fully responsive format, optimized for smartphone, PC, tablet	Real-time updates combined with push notifications (WSM, chat, email)
Expanding Support Networks	Broadly accessible yet well-referenced; simplified for the intended audience when necessary	Technically precise yet easy to understand when appropriate	Large-scale push toward potential supporters; targeted outreach for expert audiences via WSM
Announcing Initiatives	Designed to promote new projects, events, or actions	Rich in content and media elements, without excess; visually engaging	Targeted distribution on the most suitable platforms (Instagram, X, Telegram); supported by push notifications
Launching petitions	Focused and aligned with the specific goals of the petition	Concise, impactful, and action-oriented	Dedicated petition platforms (e.g., *Change.org*, *ipetitions, avaaz. org*) supported by push actions (chat, email, WSM)

4.3   Selecting the Right Influencer

In the field of DPA, an influencer is an individual with strong online visibility and thematic credibility who can shape public conversation, amplify advocacy messages, and engage digital communities around policy or regulatory issues. Through social media platforms and other digital channels, influencers can help organizations reach target stakeholders, build public support, and indirectly influence decision-making processes in the digital policy arena. As we observed during the analysis of digital relations (see Figure 2.4), influencers play a visible role. We will now focus on selecting the most suitable influencer to support the achievement of our specific objective.

4.3.1 Key Criteria for Selecting an Influencer in Digital Public Affairs

When identifying a suitable influencer for a DPA strategy, it is essential to assess a set of core characteristics. These criteria ensure that the selected individual aligns with institutional values and can contribute effectively to advocacy efforts. The following dimensions are particularly relevant:

- **Ethics.** From an ethical standpoint, no exceptions are permissible. The influencer must demonstrate behavior aligned with the values and standards required for public engagement and must never have directly or indirectly supported activities that violate moral or ethical norms. Evaluation levels:
  - *Clear*: ethics is a non-negotiable criterion. A person either meets ethical standards or does not.
  - *Unclear*: in cases of ambiguity or past behavior that raises concerns, the individual should be considered unsuitable.

- **Institutional Affinity.** The ideal influencer should be capable of engaging with institutions. This means having a credible public profile and a willingness to interact with institutional stakeholders. We define four levels of institutional affinity:
  - *High*: recognized by institutional actors as credible and capable of constructive dialogue.
  - *Medium*: possesses characteristics suitable for institutional engagement, but with limited experience in this area.
  - *Low*: no significant negative factors, but lacks evident strengths in institutional interaction.
  - *None*: not considered suitable for institutional relations.

- **Thematic Affinity.** The closer the influencer's expertise is to the subject of the advocacy campaign, the more effective the collaboration will be. However, this criterion often reduces the available pool. Balancing popularity and subject matter relevance is key. Assessment levels:
  - *High*: has previously expressed credible and relevant opinions on the subject matter.
  - *Medium*: recognized as authoritative in one or more sectors, with only indirect or partial relevance to the target issue.
  - *Low*: no meaningful correlation between the influencer's expertise and the campaign's theme.
  - *None*: the influencer's image and content are misaligned or incompatible with the topic.

- **Stability.** Partnering with an influencer who lacks long-term relevance poses a reputational and strategic risk. Preference should be given to individuals with a well-established presence and continued relevance over time.
  Stability is measured by years of consistent, high-impact activity:

  - *High*: five years or more.
  - *Medium*: between one and five years.
  - *Low*: between six months and one year.
  - *None*: less than six months.

- **Results.** Performance metrics are central to evaluating influencers. While there is no universal benchmark due to the diversity of digital domains, companies should define KPIs relevant to their goals and assess candidates accordingly. Performance is categorized as:

  - *High*: demonstrated impact aligned with the company's predefined KPIs.
  - *Medium*: mid-range performance relative to the established evaluation framework.
  - *Low*: performance falls significantly short of expectations.
  - *None*: lack of measurable track record. Self-declared potential without data is not considered sufficient.

- **Follower Count and Engagement.** The number of followers, combined with engagement metrics (such as interaction rates), remains a key indicator of influence. As with performance, companies should set quantitative thresholds based on campaign needs. Levels of assessment:

  - *High*: large, active follower base exceeding expectations.
  - *Medium*: follower and engagement metrics within an acceptable range.
  - *Low*: one or both indicators significantly below the expected benchmark.
  - *None*: absence of verifiable data on followers or engagement.

The evaluation scales presented above enable a preliminary quantitative assessment of an influencer's suitability for DPA activities. A simple scoring system is applied: 3 points for *high*, 2 for *medium*, and 1 for *low*. The *ethics* criterion is treated as a prerequisite and scored separately, with a value of 100 for verified ethical integrity and 0 in cases of uncertainty. This ensures that only individuals with a clearly positive ethical standing are considered, effectively filtering out unsuitable candidates from the outset. The remaining criteria can then be assessed numerically, allowing for straightforward comparison across multiple candidates. **The resulting scores typically fall within a range of 0 to 15.**

However, the final score should not be interpreted mechanically. It serves as a **general indicator**, useful for ranking and filtering, but must be complemented by a qualitative interpretation to fully grasp the influencer's strategic fit for the specific objectives of a DPA initiative.

Let's consider an example: imagine two influencers each receive a total score of 11. On the surface, they may appear equally suitable. Yet, a closer look reveals very different profiles. As illustrated in Figure 4.1, their scores can be visualized using a radar chart, which makes it immediately evident that their strengths and weaknesses diverge significantly. This scenario allows us to introduce two common influencer archetypes in DPA:

- **the Guru:** a subject-matter expert with strong institutional credibility and thematic authority, yet limited social media presence. In the DPA context, this could be a respected academic, scientist, or policy professional, highly influential in policy circles but not widely known to the general public. Their value lies in depth, not reach.
- **The Star:** an individual with a strong social media following and high engagement levels, but limited thematic relevance or institutional credibility. While their popularity can be leveraged for visibility, their effectiveness in influencing policy or engaging with institutions may be more limited.

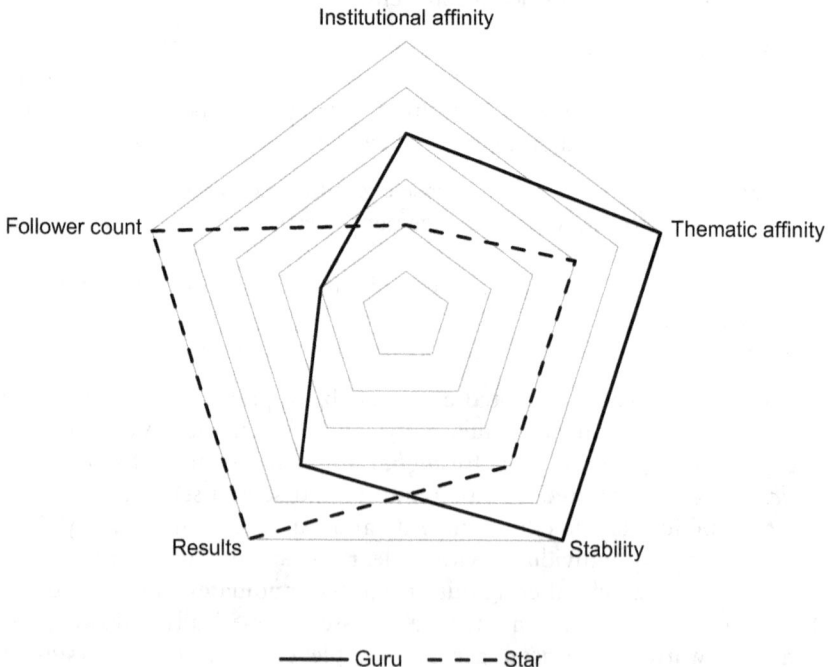

Figure 4.1 Influencer: Guru versus Star.

The diagram in Figure 4.1 provides an effective tool for immediate comparison, enabling us to focus on the most relevant elements for a campaign and rapidly narrow down the most suitable candidates. While a wide spectrum of intermediate profiles exists between the two extremes, the archetypes presented – **Guru** and **Star** – represent clear and emblematic reference points for strategic decision-making.

In the overall evaluation, we will consider varying scores for candidates aligned with these two categories. The assessment format can be summarized as follows:

- **Guru (x)** with possible plus/minus indicators
- **Star (x)** with possible plus/minus indicators

The **x** in parentheses indicates the score assigned on a scale from 0 to 15 (assuming the ethical score of 100 is already met). The **plus/minus** qualifier refers to a standout trait that is not typical of the profile but adds strategic value. For instance, a high-performing *Star* who also demonstrates a strong capacity for institutional engagement may be evaluated as: *Star (12) + Institutional Affinity*.

4.4 Synergic Planning of Traditional and DPA Activities

In the management of DPA – as with traditional Public Affairs – some activities must be handled on an ad hoc basis, often requiring immediate response, while others call for the development of structured, long-term intervention programs aimed at achieving strategic objectives. Particularly in the latter case, it becomes essential to **build synergies between the traditional and digital domains**. To act effectively, one must develop a **coherent timeline** that integrates activities and deadlines across both types of intervention.

WSM tools should be appropriately calibrated to serve a dual function: **supporting traditional PA actions** and **managing the digital relationships** that arise alongside them. In practice, we will observe a combination of "real-world" and "virtual" interactions. However, the effects of digital interactions will often materialize in the real world as well, making it crucial to monitor and leverage the online channel.

Each action may be either pre-planned or reactive, depending on whether it originates from internal strategy or is triggered by third-party initiatives. Let's recall a classification of traditional PA actions based on the primary action involved:

- **Planned Action:** designed and scheduled for short or medium-term implementation.

- **Adverse Action:** an initiative – either anticipated or unforeseen – originating from third-party actors. It may also be a reaction to one of our previous activities.
- **Reaction to Adverse Action:** a countermeasure adopted by the company in response to an adverse action.

Section 4.4 will examine the strategic and operational approaches for managing adverse digital actions, particularly at the WSM (post) level.

Now, to better understand how **online tools can be used in synergy with traditional efforts**, let's examine a case involving a planned action. In this context, **WSM** tools can serve three distinct **strategic functions:**

- **Pre-Positioning:** WSM tools are highly effective in generating attention and building anticipation around a specific issue, stakeholder, or upcoming event. Their use can be strategically planned in the run-up to an initiative to shape perception and set the narrative.
- **Message Amplification:** during the execution phase of a planned initiative or event, WSM platforms enable the rapid and wide dissemination of messages, enhancing real-time visibility and engagement. The effectiveness of this phase is strongly influenced by the perceived relevance and newsworthiness of the topic.
- **Sustained Engagement:** after the conclusion of an action, it may be strategically useful to prolong attention, reinforce key messages, or lay the groundwork for future advocacy. WSM tools allow for the continuation of the conversation and help keep the issue alive in the public and institutional sphere over time.

Imagine that we anticipate a **positive and strategically relevant event** occurring at time t_0 for example, a favorable public statement made by a political figure aligned with our objectives. This scenario is illustrated in the first row of Table 4.3.

We begin by **pre-positioning** for the event. As shown in the table, at t_{-2} we initiate a WSM information campaign $\left(\text{WSM}_y = \textbf{Content diffusion}\right)$, followed by a pre-announcement at t_{-1}, where we signal the imminent release of the official statement $\left(\text{WSM}_{y+1} = \textbf{Initiative launch}\right)$. At the actual moment the statement is made $\left(t_0\right)$, we communicate it widely through digital channels $\left(\text{WSM}_y = \textbf{Content diffusion}\right)$.

In the subsequent phase $\left(t+1\right)$, we maintain the flow of information and **enrich the narrative**, highlighting progress and implications derived from the announcement $\left(\text{WSM}_{y+2} = \textbf{Narrative construction}\right)$. From $t+2$ onward, we resume **consensus-building activities** $\left(\text{WSM}_{y+3}\right)$, which may have already been initiated at $t-3$ (not shown in the table), and we continue them until a tangible outcome is achieved, such as the adoption of a favorable measure in line with the original political statement.

Table 4.3 WSM Activities Supporting a Traditional Public Affairs Action

	t_{-2}	t_{-1}	t_0	t_{+1}	t_{+2}
Planned action X	= =	= =	**Favorable public statement**	= =	= =
WSM$_y$	Content diffusion	= =	Content diffusion	Content diffusion	= =
WSM$_{y+1}$	= =	Initiative launch	= =	= =	= =
WSM$_{y+2}$	= =	= =	= =	Narrative construction	Narrative construction
WSM$_{y+3}$	= =	= =	= =	= =	Consensus generation

In Table 4.3, each specific WSM action type is consistently positioned in the same row for clarity. For example, Content diffusion always corresponds to WSM$_y$. This simplified visualization is useful for macro-level planning. However, in a detailed execution plan, it may be necessary to differentiate between multiple content dissemination efforts, even if they serve the same strategic function. In that case, rather than referring generically to WSM$_y$, we would distinguish separate actions such as WSM$_y$, WSM$_{y+x}$, and WSM$_{y+k}$, each assigned its own row to reflect its unique role and timing within the campaign.

In the context of an advocacy project, it is common to use a **Gantt chart** that incorporates both **offline** (real-world) activities and **WSM** actions. To complement the traditional timeline, it is useful to include **milestones** that mark significant external events, which may influence or require adjustments to the WSM plan.

This timeline should also account for **reactions to third-party initiatives**, both offline and online. The format used – whether tabular or graphical – should be selected based on the project's complexity, duration, the number of actions planned, and their frequency. Although it is technically possible to include **WSM actions initiated by external actors**, doing so may increase the complexity of the plan and lead to excessive time spent on analysis. Therefore, this inclusion should be carefully evaluated and remain functional and streamlined.

Table 4.4 illustrates a standard **Action Plan format**. The upper section shows the primary WSM activities, while the lower section outlines the traditional components: direct actions, adverse events, and reactive measures. The layout is highly flexible: it consists of two coordinated tables, where new initiatives can be added to the lower section while the upper section remains fixed and advances according to defined time intervals (T_i). The plan starts from the project's inception (T_0) and can be visualized over

Table 4.4 WSM Action Plan

	T0	T1	T2	T3	T4	T5
WEB AND SOCIAL + MEDIA ACTIONS						
Content dissemination	In support of action P1	= =	In support of action P1	In support of action P1	= =	= =
Building Credibility and Generating Consensus	= =	= =	= =	= =	In support of action P1	In support of action P1
Narrative Construction and Storytelling	= =	= =	= =	In support of action P1	In support of action P1	= =
Creating Digital Hubs	= =	= =	= =	= =	= =	= =
Expanding Support Networks	= =	= =	= =	= =	= =	In support of reactive action R1
Announcing initiatives	= =	In support of action P1	= =	= =	In contrast to adverse action K1	= =
Launching petitions	= =	= =	= =	= =	= =	= =
TRADITIONAL ACTIONS						
Planned action P1	= =	= =	Public statement	= =	= =	= =
Planned action P2	= =	= =	Public statement	= =	= =	= =
Adverse action K1	= =	= =	= =	Adverse public statement	= =	= =
Reactive action R1	= =	= =	= =	= =	= =	= =

select time intervals $(T_x - T_{x+n})$ as the initiative evolves. **Blank cells** indicate actions not scheduled or not relevant within the observed time frame.

4.5 Institutional Crisis Management in the Digital Sphere

In the context of a reputational or institutional crisis, communication is never a neutral act. Every message – or deliberate silence – carries strategic weight and relational consequences. In DPA, choosing whether, how, and when to communicate becomes a critical decision, especially when institutional actors are unlikely to support a company's position that may disadvantage key stakeholders or voting constituencies.

Let us consider a case where the company has already taken action behind closed doors to protect its institutional relationships and assert its position. From this starting point, we can explore a range of DPA communication strategies, each with distinct implications and levels of exposure:

- **Non-communication:** while potentially perceived as an implicit admission of guilt, it may be a conscious choice aimed at avoiding further escalation, particularly when silent diplomacy has already been pursued.
- **Channel selection:** even when the company's position is grounded in sound economic reasoning, selecting the right communication platform is essential to limit distortions and polarization.
- **Content selection:** not all aspects of a situation need to be disclosed equally. Strategic message curation is necessary to safeguard relationships while still conveying key elements of the company's stance.
- **Timing:** timing is often decisive. A well-timed message – aligned with channel and content – can maximize impact. Some communications require immediacy, while others demand patience and precision.
- **Radical Transparency:** the opposite of non-communication, this approach entails full openness and exposure. It can be powerful but also risky and should be used only when fully aligned with broader strategic goals.
- **Communication Agreement:** when there is alignment with institutional actors, it may be possible to coordinate on *what*, *how*, and *when* to communicate, effectively negotiating a shared public position.
- **Delegation:** if an intermediary has represented the company, public communication can be entrusted entirely to that actor. In some cases, the delegate may even be a public institution itself.

Table 4.5 summarizes how different DPA tools can be applied according to each of these strategic choices.

Table 4.5 Digital Public Affairs for Crisis Management

	Traditional Media	Web	Social Media	Chat and Mail
Non-communication	= =	= =	= =	Only toward institutions
Channel Selection	Based on impact, topic, and geographical relevance	Use corporate/institutional websites if the issue is highly significant	Prioritize platforms already used by the institution	Email for official responses
Content Selection	Clear, analytical, and consistent with institutional framing	Replicate the official company position	Assertive, focused posts; avoid public disputes or unnecessary multimedia	Avoid short chat replies; prefer clear, well-structured emails
Timing	Avoid proactive messaging in the short term; reassess later	Immediate, if appropriate; avoid re-addressing unless strictly necessary	Respond promptly when required; avoid delays, repetition, or untimely interactions	Prioritize accuracy over speed (in chats); slower email replies are acceptable
Radical Transparency	Possible to rely on one channel only	One or more official digital channels	Provide full content promptly; limit to one platform if needed; selective replies are acceptable	Secondary channel; can be used for accurate and well-crafted messages
Communication Agreement	Use pre-agreed media outlets	Prefer the institution/intermediary to make the announcement	Follow agreed framework; likes, shares, and reactions are not strategic	Usually not needed, except for service-related or technical replies
Delegation	Channel choice entrusted to the delegate	Use delegate's official or news-based channels	Delegate may use social media at their discretion, based on usual practice	Responses handled by delegate or company, depending on relationship with the sender

4.6   Select the Most Effective Channel

Let us now examine the most effective communication channels for engaging with institutional counterparts, based on the **level of interest and urgency** that a particular issue holds for both parties. Traditional in-person meetings are not included in this analysis, as the objective is to identify alternative or complementary communication methods that offer greater flexibility and immediacy.

In Table 4.6, the rows represent the most relevant combinations of shared interest and urgency, each categorized as **high, medium, or low**. The columns list potential communication channels and key considerations for selecting the most appropriate method of contact.

In the **first row**, we find the scenario in which both parties – company and institution – share **high urgency and high interest** in the matter. The relationship is close, and both sides are actively working together to maximize responsiveness and impact. In such cases, **formality gives way to immediacy**, and the most direct communication channels are preferred, such as instant messaging apps or traditional phone calls.

The **second row** captures a different scenario: both parties share a **high level of interest**, but the matter is **not urgent** and does not pose any immediate problem. Here, the expectation of a response from the institutional counterpart is reasonable, and without time constraints, the choice of communication channel can be made with more calm and flexibility.

The **medium case** refers to situations that are still evolving or of potential relevance but have **not yet become a priority** for either party. Urgency remains undefined and communication should be measured – neither too frequent nor too informal – while always keeping the recipient's preferences and attention level in mind. Should a significant contextual event arise or the company decides to take a firm position, the perceived relevance of the issue may change accordingly.

In the **last row**, both parties consider the issue **low in interest and urgency**. In such cases, any preferred communication channel may be used **and no feedback may be expected or even required**.

Two particularly interesting cases are those presented in the third and fifth rows of Table 4.6. Although they may seem conceptually similar, they reveal substantial differences upon closer examination. In the first case (third row of Table 4.6), the issue is of high importance to us, while the counterpart appears to regard it as of medium or low relevance. In such situations, it is essential to convey the significance of the matter as effectively as possible. A verbal explanation is generally the most appropriate channel, comprehensive, detailed, and inclusive of all key elements necessary to fully grasp the issue and its underlying urgency. At the same time, it is important to manage our own urgency and avoid placing undue pressure when seeking a response. In the second case (fifth row of Table 4.6),

Table 4.6 Selecting the Communication Channel Based on Interest and Urgency

Interest and Urgency	Appropriate Channels	Contact Frequency	Form of Communication	Notes
High shared interest and urgent	All channels, with a prevalence of instant messaging and voice calls	High (within hours or minutes)	Unstructured and informal	Communication occurs across multiple channels to achieve the desired outcome as quickly as possible
High shared interest but not urgent	Channel choice is flexible until the issue becomes more defined	Low (every few days)	Comprehensive and extensive	The topic may remain in this state or shift toward urgency or diminished interest over time
High interest (not shared) and urgent	Mixed channels, with an emphasis on voice communication	Medium (within several hours or a day)	Clear and concise	Messages should be direct and outcome-oriented, potentially delivered through presentations or succinct updates
Medium interest and urgency	Email and messaging platforms	Medium (within a day or so)	Structured and cordial	Typically a phase of analysis or observation, helping prevent escalation into high- or low-interest situations
Low interest (not shared) and urgent	Email and call	Medium to low (hours to days)	Comprehensive and formal	A sensitive scenario where urgency is perceived by only one party; avoid overwhelming the recipient with excessive messaging
Low shared interest and not urgent	Email or traditional mail	Low (several days to a week)	Simple and somewhat informal	Can be addressed alongside other communications or during in-person meetings when convenient

the situation is reversed: the matter is of low interest to us but is perceived as important by the counterpart. Here, it is vital to show responsiveness and readiness to engage with the topic. While it may not be a priority for us, we must demonstrate willingness to cooperate. However, it is equally important to avoid elevating a secondary matter above more strategically relevant issues currently being handled with the institution.

To effectively manage institutional communication in these circumstances, a few core principles should be followed:

- **Avoid Unnecessary Pressure:** it is important to manage the anxiety that may arise from delayed responses. Institutions should never feel that communication efforts are becoming invasive or coercive. Consistency, moderation, and composure must characterize the interaction. If a response is not forthcoming, it signals the need to rethink and adjust the strategy. There will always be other stakeholders who can be approached to advance the objective. Sending compulsive or repeated messages is counterproductive and can damage the relationship without improving outcomes.
- **Ensure Reciprocal Responsiveness:** institutional counterparts must always receive appropriate responses to their inquiries. The choice of timing and communication channels should be tailored to the nature of the exchange. For instance, a text message may suffice for logistical updates (such as scheduling or brief follow-ups), but it is unsuitable for discussing complex matters. Even when declining a request, the response should be articulated clearly and respectfully, preferably in person and well-justified. A "no" communicated via text is never acceptable in the context of professional PA work.

While relationships tend to evolve and become more fluid over time, it is essential to **maintain a professional tone**. Familiarity should not lead to informality that could compromise the relationship's integrity. Messaging can be a useful tool for maintaining contact, but excessive or overly casual use can foster a false sense of closeness. It is advisable to always calibrate the frequency and tone of messaging to suit the nature of the relationship.

4.7 Managing Hostile Posts

The key attributes of a post were outlined in Section 4.1. Here, we focus specifically on the elements to consider when dealing with a hostile post. A single post can convey multiple messages, some explicit, others subtle or implicit. It is therefore essential to determine whether the message is generally adverse or specifically directed at our organization.

With this necessary premise, let us consider the scenario in which a hostile post is published by a relevant figure in response to a position expressed by our company. The **first rule** is to **avoid reacting immediately**, even when we have the authority and information needed to respond. Impulsive or poorly considered reactions must be avoided. A hostile message must be carefully analyzed before planning any response. This is particularly important when it comes from an institutional figure. Below are the main attributes to assess when interpreting such a post.

4.7.1   Actor

Who is the post attributed to?

- *Institution*: the post is published through the official account of an institution, representing the highest level of formality.
- *Politician (non-office holder)*: a political figure speaking in a personal capacity, without holding any institutional position.
- *Politician in office*: a political figure currently holding an official role.
- *Intermediary*: the post is published by a qualified third party, acting as a delegated spokesperson.
- *Influencer*: a well-known figure, not institutionally recognized, acting as an informal intermediary.
- *Other*: this category includes all remaining cases, including anonymous posts or those published in unclear or chaotic contexts.

4.7.2   Genesis

What triggered the post?

- *Institutional initiative*: includes both scheduled communications and unplanned or spontaneous publications.
- *Reaction to a company initiative*: a public, negative response to a real-world action carried out by the company, which is presumably contested.
- *Reaction to a third-party initiative*: similar to the previous case, but triggered by the action of another actor in the public sphere.
- *Response to a company post*: a hostile post published in direct reply to one of the company's own messages.
- *Response to a third-party post*: an institutional figure reacts to content published by another party, aligning themselves with that position.

4.7.3   Topic

What is the topic of the post?

- *Established and ongoing*: a well-known issue, on which positions have already been expressed, with no major developments.

- *Ongoing with updates*: the issue is familiar, but recent events or changes make further communication necessary.
- *New*: a previously known topic now entering public discourse, perhaps for the first time in connection with the institutional figure or the digital environment.
- *Occasional*: a time-limited or one-off issue tied to a specific event or situation, unlikely to evolve into a broader public matter.

4.7.4   Content Accuracy

How accurate or truthful is the information presented?

- *True*: the most common scenario, in which the content is entirely accurate.
- *False*: classic case of fake news. In institutional contexts, false posts may stem from a lack of information rather than intentional misinformation.
- *Partial*: the content is selectively presented, emphasizing certain aspects while omitting others that may weaken the argument.
- *Distorted*: accurate facts are misinterpreted or presented in a misleading way.

4.7.5   Relevance

How significant is the post?

- *High*: several factors suggest the post is important and requires monitoring or response.
- *Medium*: there is insufficient information to fully assess its importance. (Note: This rating should be used sparingly, and only when necessary.)
- *Low*: the post is considered to have little or no relevance, and no further action is required.

We have introduced a wide range of parameters for assessing hostile posts. However, in practical application, **only a subset of these variables will typically be considered** when making decisions. For illustrative and didactic purposes, we will now take into account all the attributes listed so far and offer some reflections to support effective decision-making.

To facilitate this analysis, we introduce the concept of **Attention Level**, understood as an estimate of the relevance attributed to each variable. In Table 4.7, each variable used to classify a hostile post is assigned an attention level, on a scale from **1 (minimal)** to **4 (maximum)**.

At first glance, one might assume that a level 4 score automatically requires a response. This is not necessarily the case. High values (such as 3 or 4) call for careful consideration, but do not by themselves dictate a

Table 4.7 Attention Levels for Hostile Post Attributes

Hostile Post Attributes	Attention Level
Actor	
Institution	4
Politician in office	3
Politician (not in office)	3
Intermediary	2
Influencer	1
Other	1
Genesis	
Institution initiative	4
Reaction to a company initiative	4
Reaction to a third-party initiative	1
Response to a company post	3
Response to a third-party post	1
Topic	
Established and ongoing	1
Ongoing with updates	4
New	3
Occasional	2
Content Accuracy	
True	4
False	3
Partial	1
Misinterpreted (Distorted)	2
Relevance	
High	4
Medium	2
Low	1

specific course of action. Conversely, low scores (1 or 2) do not automatically justify ignoring the post. They simply suggest a lower level of immediate concern.

In operational terms, when assessing a hostile post, it is useful to assign an **Attention Level** to each attribute (such as *actor*, *genesis*, *topic*, etc.) in order to calculate an overall score. This cumulative score – ranging from a **minimum of 5** to a **maximum of 20** – serves as a preliminary indicator of the post's potential impact.

Depending on the total value, the post can be initially classified as follows:

- **Modest interest:** total score between **5 and 7**
- **Routine management:** total score between **8 and 14**
- **Need for further investigation:** total score between **15 and 20**

This indicator does not replace analytical judgment, but rather supports it by offering a structured framework for prioritization and action planning.

4.7.6 Genesis-Actor Matrix and Topic-Content Matrix

The attributes presented in Table 4.7 can occur in various combinations, each carrying different levels of significance and potentially pointing to a medium-term strategic intent on the part of the subject involved. These combinations must always be interpreted in light of the broader informational context. In this section, we analyze two key sets of relationships: those between **Genesis and Actor**, and those between **Topic and Content**. The **Relevance** attribute is considered separately, as it represents a composite indicator that already provides a synthetic judgment of the post's importance.

Let us begin with the combination of **Genesis and Actor.** To explore this relationship, we construct a two-dimensional graph in which *Genesis* values are plotted along the x-axis and *Actor* values along the y-axis. Given that these attributes are rated on a 1-to-4 scale, we can broadly divide them into two ranges: **1–2** (low impact, exploratory dimension) and **3–4** (high impact, declarative dimension). These values are assigned according to the scoring system detailed in Table 4.7. The result is a **2×2 matrix**, represented in Figure 4.2, which systematizes the combinations and helps guide interpretation.

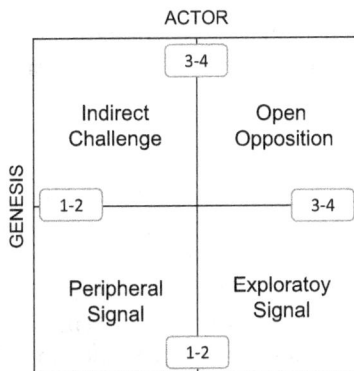

Figure 4.2 Genesis-actor matrix.

The four quadrants of the **Genesis-Actor Matrix** synthesize how the nature of the message and the identity of the actor interact in hostile communication scenarios. Each quadrant suggests a specific dynamic and potential response strategy:

- **Open Opposition** (*Genesis: 3–4; Actor: 3–4*). This is the most direct and high-impact configuration: an institutional or highly authoritative actor openly and deliberately challenges our position. Such a situation cannot be ignored or downplayed and usually demands prompt and well-considered action.
- **Indirect Challenge** (*Genesis: 1–2; Actor: 3–4*). This is the classic scenario described earlier in this manual, where a relatively marginal message is subsequently endorsed or amplified by an institutional actor. While we refer to it as an *indirect challenge*, it describes a concerted communication move designed to legitimize a position indirectly, often through WSM strategies.
- **Exploratory Signal** (*Genesis: 3–4; Actor: 1–2*). In this quadrant, the content of the post suggests a strong position, yet it is disseminated by a non-institutional or marginal actor. This often indicates a **tactical delegation**, a cautious attempt by institutional stakeholders to test the waters without exposing themselves directly. It can serve exploratory or destabilizing purposes, such as probing public sentiment or preparing the ground for future escalation.
- **Peripheral Signal** (*Genesis: 1–2; Actor: 1–2*). This scenario is initially comparable to **background noise**: the message comes from a marginal actor and refers to an issue of limited or unclear importance. Unless corroborating signals emerge, posts in this quadrant can generally be deprioritized.

Using a similar methodology, we now analyze the combination of **Topic** and **Content Accuracy**, resulting in the matrix, shown in Figure 4.3. The four quadrants represent different interpretative scenarios, each with distinct implications for monitoring and response strategies:

- **Heightened Attention** (*Topic: 3–4; Content: 3–4*). This configuration indicates a situation that demands heightened attention. The messages are both substantial in content and focused on emerging or evolving topics. They likely express positions that diverge from our own and may signal an escalation or a shift in tone.
- **Emerging Risk** (*Topic: 3–4; Content: 1–2*). This scenario may represent a potential threat, as it involves new or sensitive topics that are communicated in a misleading or unfavorable way. These messages may function as **early warning signals**, suggesting the possibility of reputational or operational challenges.

CONTENT ACCURACY

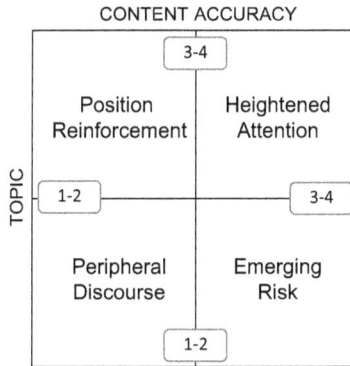

Figure 4.3 Topic-content accuracy matrix.

- **Position Reinforcement** (*Topic: 1–2; Content: 3–4*). This quadrant includes posts that reiterate well-established positions or reaffirm already known narratives. They may also subtly introduce **corollary arguments**, reinforcing a broader discourse without presenting radically new information.
- **Peripheral Discourse** (*Topic: 1–2; Content: 1–2*). Posts in this category are typically weak in both topical novelty and content accuracy. They may rehash familiar themes, reinterpret past issues, or loosely reference current events. While generally low impact, such posts can contribute to **background noise** or be used tactically to **shift attention**.

The two matrices, although based on different variables, should lead to consistent results. This **redundancy is intended to reduce the risk of error**.

4.7.7   Decision-Making Framework for Reactions

Once the problem setting is complete, the next step is to define the most appropriate course of action. This step involves two tasks. First, you must evaluate the possible forms of reaction. Second, you need to assess the impact each option could have on institutional and reputational relationships. In Section 4.4, we introduced the concept of post genesis from a planning perspective; we now revisit this theme to develop a structured response methodology. Depending on the specific circumstances and context, **four primary reaction strategies** can be identified:

- **Adverse response:** assertively restate the company's position, while contextualizing it with respect to the elements contained in the hostile post. This approach is direct and often confrontational, but may be necessary to defend strategic priorities.

- **Conciliatory response**: highlight aspects that allow for de-escalation or mediation, with the aim of avoiding a public confrontation. This may involve introducing new information, suggesting delays, or inviting further discussion in a private setting.
- **Reserved response (no WSM)**: what may appear to be a non-response is, in reality, a deliberate choice to **protect the institutional relationship.** While this may entail reputational costs in the digital arena, it is used when the preservation of a working relationship with the institutional actor takes precedence. In such cases, the response is provided privately, preferably in person or via direct communication, without engaging in online discourse.
- **No response**: opting not to respond is typical when the issue is deemed either **insignificant** or **strategically risky**, particularly if a reply could trigger a broader and potentially damaging public debate.

Each of these reactions comes with trade-offs, and none is without consequence. The choice must be weighed carefully. We operate in an environment that is similar to traditional media exposure. However, there is a key difference: on social media, anyone can join the conversation. This can alter its course in unpredictable ways.

Table 4.8 outlines the rationale behind each possible response, including associated risks and recommendations for when each option may be appropriate.

At this stage, we have at our disposal two analytical tools – Figure 4.2 (GA Matrix) and Figure 4.3 (TC Matrix) – which allow us to **classify the nature of a hostile post.** We also add a typology of potential responses, presented in Table 4.8. Together, these elements form a framework. This framework supports a structured and consistent approach to decision-making in the face of digital hostility.

We begin by addressing posts that fall into the *Peripheral Signal* or *Peripheral Discourse* quadrants. These are generally characterized by low relevance and limited potential impact. In most cases, they can be deprioritized and no public response is required. However, exceptions may apply depending on specific **corporate policies** regarding digital engagement (e.g., systematic replies to all mentions) or in the presence of extraordinary circumstances.

Our attention then shifts to the **combinations involving the remaining three quadrants** of the matrices. These represent more complex and potentially sensitive scenarios that call for a calibrated response. Table 4.9 outlines the possible pairings of matrix positions and associates them with the most appropriate types of reaction. A dedicated *Notes* column offers brief operational guidance to support decision-making in context-specific cases.

Table 4.8 Types of Reaction to Hostile Posts

Reaction	Rationale	Risk	Recommendation
Adverse response	Clearly assert the company's position	Potential strain on institutional relationships	Use only as part of a structured strategy; avoid spontaneous or emotional reactions
Conciliatory response	Keep negotiation channels open	Risk of confusing or weakening the company's positioning	Useful to de-escalate, encourage dialogue, and prevent public confrontation
Reserved response	Preserve the institutional relationship	Exposure to attacks on WSM channels without the possibility to respond	Recommended when further dialogue with the counterpart is needed
No response	Message deemed irrelevant or counterproductive to engage	Silence may be misinterpreted or exploited; issue may escalate	Avoid exposure when topics or actors lack relevance or credibility

Table 4.9 Strategic Framework for Responding to Hostile Posts

GA/TC Combination		Reaction	Note
Open Opposition	**Position Reinforcement**	*Defined strategy*	Follow the strategic guidelines established by the PA function
Open Opposition	**Heightened Attention**	Adverse or conciliatory response	A public stance is advisable; whether to escalate or contain should be evaluated case by case
Open Opposition	**Emerging Risk**	Adverse response	Timely intervention is recommended to clarify the company's position and avoid ambiguity
Indirect Challenge	**Position Reinforcement**	*Defined strategy*	Follow the strategic guidelines established by the PA function

(Continued)

Table 4.9 (Continued)

GA/TC Combination		Reaction	Note
Indirect Challenge	**Heightened Attention**	Reserved response	A private discussion with the institutional actor may be appropriate; future engagement remains possible
Indirect Challenge	**Emerging Risk**	No response	The post does not warrant special attention; responding may increase unnecessary exposure
Exploratory Signal	**Position Reinforcement**	No response	The message is a weak reiteration and generally does not require a formal response
Exploratory Signal	**Heightened Attention**	Reserved response	A direct clarification request to the institution is appropriate, without engaging third parties
Exploratory Signal	**Emerging Risk**	–	This scenario is included for theoretical completeness but is highly unlikely in practice

4.8   Artificial Intelligence for Public Affairs

Throughout the book, the potential use of AI in the tools discussed has been consistently referenced. However, this section aims to provide a unified overview to foster a comprehensive understanding of how AI is applied in PA. The paragraph begins with an analysis of current applications of AI, continues with an exploration of potential future developments, and concludes with an examination of the inherent challenges of AI, which also impact the field of institutional relations.

4.8.1   Current Applications of AI in Public Affairs

AI technologies are already being applied to a range of PA activities. Key use cases include:

- **Stakeholder Mapping and Network Analysis:** AI significantly enhances the identification and analysis of stakeholder networks related to specific policy issues. By processing large volumes of data – including regulations, public records, and social media content – machine learning can uncover key influencers, decision-makers, and the nature of their connections.

  Advanced PA platforms incorporate these capabilities into comprehensive databases of institutional actors and intermediaries, enabling strategic relationship management. Automating this process allows professionals to swiftly identify the most relevant stakeholders and understand their interdependencies, a critical asset for effective engagement.

  Referring to the tools in this category discussed throughout the text, **AI proves especially useful** for creating and updating the following:

  - Institutional Stakeholder Profile (see Figure 2.1).
  - Institutional Relationship Map (see Figure 2.3).
  - Framework for analyzing the role of institutions and intermediaries (see Table 2.2 and Table 2.3).
  - Web, Social, and Media Relationship Map (see Figure 2.4).
  - Hidden Relationships (see Figure 2.5).
  - Relational Risk Profile (see Figure 3.4).

- **Policy Monitoring and Legislative Tracking:** One of the most widespread uses of AI in PA is monitoring the policy landscape in real time. AI-powered systems can automatically collect and analyze legislative and regulatory information from numerous sources – legislative proposal/bills, government websites, meeting minutes, etc. – far faster than any human team. These tools use natural language processing (NLP) to categorize and tag proposals by topic, assess their relevance, and even predict the likelihood of a proposal's passage. Advanced platforms will not only alert practitioners to a new bill or regulation but also summarize its contents and assess its potential impact.

  This important activity is primarily linked to the *Public Affairs Technical Tool* related to *Regulation Issuance* (see Table 3.3).

- **Sentiment Analysis and Public Opinion Tracking:** In the realm of DPA, AI is employed to gauge public sentiment on policy issues and stakeholder opinions at scale. Techniques like sentiment analysis (using NLP to determine if text is positive, negative, or neutral) allow practitioners to monitor how the public or specific communities feel about a pending policy or a company's advocacy campaign. Similarly, AI-driven media monitoring tools track online news and social media in multiple languages, helping PA teams detect emerging issues or shifts in public opinion early. This insight guides lobbyists in adjusting their strategy or messaging; for instance, if sentiment analysis shows growing public concern over an environmental issue, a company's PA team might proactively address those concerns in their communications.

With reference to the tools discussed, AI can therefore provide valuable support in:

- Building Decision Support Reports (see Section 2.6)
- Sentiment Overview Report (see Figure 2.9)
- Company, Antagonists and Context Actions (see Figure 2.10)
- Launching the First Post (see Tables 4.1 and 4.2)
- WSM Activities Supporting a Traditional Public Affairs Action (see Table 4.3)
- Attention Levels for Hostile Post Attributes (see Table 4.7)

- **Strategic Communication and Content Creation:** AI is also beginning to assist with crafting and targeting messages in lobbying campaigns. Generative AI models can draft first versions of policy briefs, speeches, or advocacy emails, which practitioners then refine. Some PA software includes features to automatically compile outreach emails or social media posts tailored to different audiences. AI can analyze what messages have resonated in the past and suggest optimized content (e.g., highlighting key phrases likely to engage a certain policymaker based on their record). In addition, AI-powered analytics can help target communications by identifying which stakeholders should receive a particular message.
- This AI functionality is particularly valuable for the development of *Public Affairs Relationship Tools* (see Table 3.6).

4.8.2   The Future of AI in Public Affairs

Looking ahead, AI is poised to further transform PA in several ways. As the technology matures, we can expect:

- **Predictive Policy Modeling:** AI's predictive analytics capabilities are expected to advance significantly. Researchers are developing models that analyze historical data and real-time signals – such as legislative co-sponsorship patterns, public sentiment, and economic indicators – to forecast the trajectory of legislative or regulatory actions. In the near future, a PA team might routinely consult an AI model to answer questions like: "*What is the probability that this bill will pass in the next session?*" or "*Which lawmakers are most likely to change their position on issue XYZ?*"

  Early versions of such predictive engines already exist. As these models incorporate more data and grow in sophistication, their accuracy is likely to improve. The widespread use of predictive modeling could also enhance strategic planning by enabling Advocacy campaigns to allocate resources more efficiently and focus on initiatives with the greatest chance of success.

- **AI-Generated Content and Personalization at Scale:** We are likely to see AI playing an increasingly important role in content creation for PA, enabling mass personalization. AI language models can make this feasible by drafting messages that reference what matters most to each recipient, drawing on data such as past statements or local concerns. In digital **Grassroots Lobbying**, organizations might use AI to tailor calls-to-action for individual supporters, increasing engagement by appealing to each person's values.
- **Real-Time Issue Tracking and Response:** Future AI will make the policy environment even more "live." Instead of monitoring developments reactively, AI could enable *continuous* issue tracking with instant analysis. For example, as soon as an amendment is introduced in committee or a key official makes an offhand remark on social media, AI systems could flag it and even assess the implications within minutes, notifying PA teams immediately. Coupled with mobile and cloud technology, this means lobbyists can respond on the fly from anywhere. AI might also leverage real-time data feeds to warn when conditions are ripe for a policy change, allowing advocates to prepare even before a proposal is formally on the table. In crisis communications or fast-moving regulatory changes, such rapid analysis could be crucial. Moreover, as NLP improves, AI assistants might be able to engage in real-time dialogue with stakeholders.
- **Simulating Policymaker Behavior through Digital Twins:** A potential use of AI-powered digital twins in PA is to simulate the behavior of key policymakers based on their past votes, public statements, and communication patterns. These digital replicas can help PA teams test messaging strategies, predict policy reactions, and refine advocacy efforts before real-world engagement. By offering realistic, data-driven simulations, digital twins can enhance strategic planning and stakeholder alignment.

Ultimately, the future of PA in the age of AI will be a blend of high-tech analytics and the timeless art of human persuasion. The most effective lobbying organizations will likely be those that can marry data-driven insights with creative, ethical advocacy strategies.

There are several areas of concern related to the use of AI, which are currently the subject of international debate regarding its evolution and application. Box 4.1 highlights the most significant issues of this kind, focusing on the risks and limitations of applying AI in PA.

Box 4.1   Limitations and Risks of Using AI in Public Affairs

The use of AI in PA comes with significant risks, some of the key concerns include:

- **Bias and Accuracy**: AI systems are only as good as the data they are trained on. If the underlying datasets contain biases (political, racial, gender, or otherwise), the AI's outputs can unknowingly perpetuate those biases. In a PA context, this might mean an algorithm unintentionally favoring certain viewpoints or stakeholders. Thus, validation by human experts remains essential. Transparency is also a challenge: many AI models operate as "black boxes" where it's unclear why the system made a given recommendation.
- **Misinformation and Ethics**: the power of AI to generate content at scale raises the risk of manipulative practices. AI-generated text, images, or deepfake videos could be used to spread disinformation that sways opinion or discredits an opponent, a tactic that falls squarely in the realm of unethical lobbying.
- **Data Privacy**: PA work often involves handling sensitive personal data or lists of supporter contacts, information on stakeholders' policy positions, or analyses of constituent opinions. Integrating AI means using this data in new ways, which introduces privacy and security concerns.
- **Reliability and Human Oversight**: AI might be fast and tireless, but it is not infallible. Overreliance on automated analysis without human cross-checking can be dangerous. Public policy is a complex arena often driven by nuance, context, and rapidly changing dynamics that AI may not fully grasp. An algorithm might interpret language in a legislative proposal very literally and miss the political subtext that a seasoned lobbyist would catch.

The role of AI will be further examined in Section 5.5 within the context of a strategic PA model.

Bibliography

Aaker J., Smith A., *The Dragonfly Effect: Quick, Effective, and Powerful Ways To Use Social Media to Drive Social Change*, Wiley, San Francisco (California), 2010.

Alemanno A., *Lobbying for Change: Find Your Voice to Create a Better Society*, Icon Books Ltd, London, 2017.

Austin L.L., *Social Media and Crisis Communication*, Routledge, New York, 2018.

Barabasi A.L., *Linked: The New Science of Networks*, Basic Books, New York, 2003.

Bochenek L.M., *Advocacy and Organizational Engagement: Redefining the Way Organizations Engage*, Emerald Publishing, Bingley, 2019.

Di Giacomo G., *Digital Public Affairs & Advocacy: From Traditional Lobbying to Blended Public Affairs*, Franco Angeli Editore, Milan, Italy, 2021.

Di Mario C., Carro M., *Digital lobbying. Gestire strategicamente le relazioni istituzionali attraverso smart data e strumenti digitali*, Carocci Editore, 2021.

Gelak D., *Lobbying and Advocacy*, TheCapitol.Net, Alexandria (Virginia), 2018.

Kerpen D., Greenbaum M., *Likeable Social Media*, Mc Graw Hill, New York, 2019.

Lipschultz J.H., *Social Media Communication: Concepts, Practices, Data, Law and Ethics*, Routledge, New York, 2020.

McDonnel L., *2025 Social Media Content Planner & Guide: With ChatGPT Tips & AI Prompts - Guaranteed better results in less time*, Orla Kelly Publishing, Cork (Ireland), 2025.

MSL Group, *The Digital and Social Media Revolution in Public Affairs: Where We Are and Where We're Going*, Reports from Brussels and Washington DC, 2016.

Sutherland K.E., *Artificial Intelligence for Strategic Communication*, Palgrave Macmillan, Basingstoke (United Kingdom), 2025.

Vaynerchuk G., *Jab, Jab, Jab, Right Hook: How to Tell Your Story in a Noisy Social World*, Harper Business, New York, 2013.

Chapter 5

Strategic Tools

5.1 Determining the Importance and Difficulty of a Relationship

We examine the most important strategic attributes used to characterize a public stakeholder: the **Importance** and the **Difficulty** of the **Relationship**. The methodologies described refer to the institution understood as an entity; however, with appropriate adaptations, they can also be applied to individuals within government bodies. At the level of the *Institutional Stakeholder Profile* (see Figure 2.1), the individual inherits the attributes of the institution to which they belong, in the same way as with the *Relational Risk Profile* (see Figure 3.4).

To estimate the potential impact an institution may have on a company, we apply a **framework** based on the following **variables**:

- **Business Impact** (b): most institutions can act as clients for a company. Through public procurement procedures, they can purchase goods and services, but they can also allocate resources that are either directly accessible (e.g., joint projects) or indirectly accessible when assigned to third parties who will place them on the market. Once a public stakeholder has been identified, it is possible to estimate – within a defined time frame – the potential total revenue that may be generated from that subject. In general, this can be expressed as the **sum of expected revenues** (b_i).

    This value may be adjusted using a parameter β, which corrects the estimate in cases where the public entity is not the direct buyer but influences or determines the purchasing decisions of others, such as citizens or businesses. In practice:

    - $\beta > 1$ if the public stakeholder is both a source of revenue and a promoter of additional purchases.
    - $\beta < 1$ if the stakeholder influences purchasing decisions but is not a direct buyer.
    - $\beta = 1$ if the stakeholder is solely a buyer.

DOI: 10.4324/9781003647829-6

More sophisticated models can be developed by individually weighting each revenue component. AI can play a particularly valuable role in this context, helping to integrate heterogeneous data sources and design customized forecasting models that enhance the precision of revenue estimates.

- **Technical Impact** (t): primarily – but not exclusively – through legislative initiatives, a public stakeholder can generate efficiencies that lead to cost savings or conversely, introduce burdens that impact production processes. Unlike the estimation of revenue, modeling efficiency requires a function that relates the economic impact resulting from a change in a **productive variable** (e_i) following the implementation of a regulation. If we expect the institution to issue several measures that could affect the efficiency of our operations within a defined time frame, the technical impact is expressed as the sum of such functions.

As in the previous case, we introduce a corrective parameter τ, which accounts for the actual role of the stakeholder in these activities. The value of τ varies as follows:

- $\tau > 1$: when the institution issues a regulation (or other type of measure) that generates a technical benefit and also actively promotes or oversees its implementation.
- $\tau = 1$: when the institution issues the regulation but does not oversee its implementation.
- $\tau < 1$: when the involvement of another actor is required to make the provision effective, regardless of the nature of that actor.

- **Relational Value** (m): the value of a relationship with an institution can thus be expressed as a function of the *Business Impact* (b) and the *Technical Impact* (t) that the stakeholder can generate, multiplied by a parameter γ, which represents the institutional **Importance** of the public entity, what we define as the **Importance of the institutional relationship**.

The functions outlined above can be expressed as follows:

$b = \beta \Sigma_i r_i$ Business Impact

$t = \tau \Sigma_i f_i (e_i)$ Technical Impact

$m = \gamma f (b, t)$ Relational Value

Let us focus on the final expression, which determines the **Relational Value** (m). This means that the value of a relationship with a public entity depends on the *Business Impact* (b) and *Technical Impact* (t) the entity can generate for the company. It also depends on the variable γ, which expresses the institutional relevance of the public actor and its capacity to generate impacts on the connected business.

As for the calculation of the function f, which depends on (b) and (t), this is a purely algebraic matter. More complex is the **determination of** γ. To this end, we break it down into its main components, that is, the **attributes of the public entity** that can be observed and allow us to assign a value:

1. **Political relevance:** indicates the institution's influence and standing within the political system during the period under consideration.
2. **Makes determinative choices for the sector:** these choices refer broadly to regulatory initiatives, financial allocations, project launches, and similar sectoral actions.
3. **Makes determinative choices in areas that impact the company:** similar to point 2, but concerns cross-cutting measures such as taxation, labor policy, etc.
4. **Participates in relevant decisions concerning the company:** this includes the institution's ability to initiate or influence decisions with a direct impact on the company, such as acquisitions, capital involvement, or financial support.
5. **Collaborates with relevant institutions:** the actor is meaningfully involved with institutions that carry out the initiatives described in points 2 and 3.
6. **Influences public opinion:** the actor exerts a notable influence on public perception through its communication efforts.

Each of the six parameters is assessed using a binary on/off approach. This yields a value scale from 0 to 6, where 0 indicates that the actor holds none of the examined levers, while 6 denotes an actor of the utmost importance.

Table 5.1 identifies four **classes of importance:** the **Specific** class includes actors that stand out for their significant role in one of the six evaluated factors (*Targeted*), while the **Significant** and **Strategic** categories represent

Table 5.1 Importance of the Relationship (γ)

γ	Relational Profile	Importance of the Relationship
0	Not relevant	None
1	Targeted	Specific
2–3	Multi-dimensional	Significant
4–6	Systemically relevant	Strategic

the most relevant actors within a given context, territory, or sector for the company. Generally, a company interacts primarily with *Specific* and *Significant* stakeholders. Only occasionally does it become necessary to engage with an institution as important as those classified as *Strategic*. As an example, this category may include the President (or an equivalent figure) of a State.

By determining the values of (b), (t), and γ for all relevant actors, we can construct a **visual map of our relationship portfolio.** If we plot the results on a Cartesian coordinate system, with expected business value on the x-axis and predicted technical benefit on the y-axis, we obtain a representation similar to Figure 5.1.

The **size of the bubbles** reflects the value of γ (with a value of zero represented as a point), while the **color** indicates the **corrective parameter:** Black when either β or τ (or both) is greater than 1, Gray when they are equal to 1, and White when both β and τ are less than 1.

Public stakeholders that generate revenue are classified as **Commercial Actors.** Those whose impact is exclusively technical appear along the y-axis and are categorized as **Enablers.** Among the entities with a dual impact, a subset exceeding a minimum value threshold is defined as **Strategic Actors.** Others, despite having both types of impact, may present more moderate values and are classified as **Balanced Actors.** Each company may define its own threshold values for (b) and (t) to demarcate the *Strategic Actor* zone.

The graphical representation may appear to suggest focusing attention on *Strategic* counterparts; however, this is not always the case. While the map provides a valuable overview and contains a wealth of important

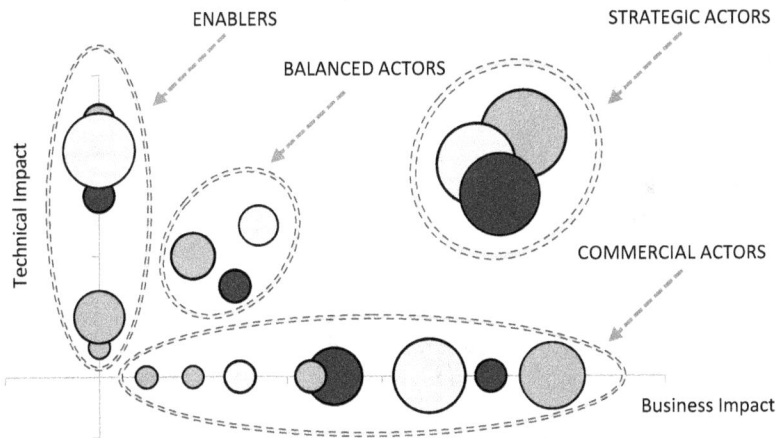

Figure 5.1 Impact map of public stakeholders.

information, the selection of a specific PA intervention should also take into account the guidance provided by the strategic tools presented later in this chapter.

Finally, it is recommended to **avoid relying solely on commercial or technical logic,** and instead to consider each actor from an institutional perspective. It is essential to remember that PA objectives do not necessarily align with those of commercial or technical functions.

5.1.1   Difficulty of a Relationship with a Public Entity

We introduce a parameter δ that captures the level of internal criticality within the institution at a given moment in time. This refers to an objective condition of complexity, which may be political, organizational, financial, or otherwise. This state is entirely independent of the relationship we may have with the institution. Therefore, **the relational difficulty we refer to is a consequence of the institution's internal complexity,** not of its interaction with the company. The preliminary analyses conducted for the development of the *Institutional Relationship Map* (see Section 2.2) are highly useful for determining δ.

Overall criticality stems not only from the severity of individual issues, but also from the simultaneous occurrence of multiple critical factors. **To determine δ,** we adopt an approach similar to that used for γ, applying a binary criterion to assess the presence or absence of each factor.

As shown in Table 5.2, three macro-categories have been identified, each containing the nine determinants of δ.

If the institution under consideration exhibits all nine critical factors, the initial value of δ is set at 9. To account for the distribution of these factors, an additional 2 points are assigned if they fall into two distinct macro-categories, and 3 points if they span across all three. This methodology allows for a δ **value ranging from 0 to a maximum of 12.**

We can now group the possible **values of δ into four distinct classes:**

- $\delta = 0$: no relevant internal criticalities are observed; the institution appears stable and fully functional.
- $\delta = 1-2$: one or more specific issues are present, all within the same category. The resulting difficulty is therefore *vertical* in nature, limited to a particular area.
- $\delta = 3-5$: the institution presents a broader level of complexity, as the criticalities are no longer isolated but interrelated.
- $\delta = 6-8$: the institution is undergoing a period of systemic change or instability.
- $\delta = 9-12$: the institution displays a high degree of structural complexity. Except in exceptional circumstances, it is not advisable to engage proactively with this actor.

Table 5.2 Difficulty of a Relationship Determinants

Macro-category	Type of Internal Criticality	Brief Description
Operational Capacity	Organizational	Internal dysfunctions, shortage of human or structural resources
	Procedural/ Bureaucratic	Slow processes, rigid procedures, lack of operational delegation
	Technological/ Infrastructural	Outdated IT systems, inadequate infrastructure, operational inefficiency
Governance and Constraints	Political	Instability, leadership transitions, conflicts between institutional levels
	Financial	Budget limitations, blocked spending, uncertainty over available funds
	Legal/Regulatory	Legal gaps, regulatory constraints, overlapping or unclear responsibilities
Institutional Culture	Resistance to Change	Opposition to reform, low adaptability to innovation
	Closure to External Stakeholders	Lack of dialogue, limited openness to companies and civil society
	Integrity and Transparency	Reputational risks, low accountability, opacity, or corruption-related issues

Table 5.3 Difficulty of a Relationship (δ)

δ	Strategic Guidance	Difficulty of the Relationship
0	Stable	Null
1–2	Focused Attention Required	Specific issue
3–5	Managed Complexity	Medium-High
6–8	High Difficulty – Strategic Caution Required	High
9–12	High-Risk Engagement	Extreme

Table 5.3 shows, for each identified δ range, the corresponding *Relational Profile* and the qualitative evaluation of the interval.

5.2   Defining the Institutional Relational Strategy

We now bring together all the variables defined so far to construct the most important strategic tool in PA: the **Institutional Positioning Matrix.**

This matrix not only provides a clear representation of the current state of institutional relationships, but also supports strategic decisions based on a clear understanding of the institutional landscape. We will then build the matrix from a corporate perspective, to assess the company's overall positioning toward public institutions.

The first step is to select the institutions on which to focus. This may include the entire relational portfolio or a subset identified according to specific criteria aligned with the strategic objective. Typically, the selection of variables such as time, location, and policy area leads to a **narrower analytical perimeter**. The most relevant PA tools to support the identification of stakeholders to be analyzed are: the *Institutional Stakeholder Profile* (see Figure 2.1), the *Institutional Relationship Map* (see Figure 2.3), and the *Impact Map of Public Stakeholders* (see Figure 5.1).

For each of the selected actors, we need to determine the following parameters:

- *Relational Risk* ρ, ranging from 1 to 9 (see Section 3.4).
- *Relationship Difficulty* δ, ranging from 0 to 12.
- *Relationship Importance* γ, ranging from 0 to 6.
- *Business Impact* (b).
- *Technical Impact* (t).

For the definition of the last four parameters, see Section 5.1. At this stage, we map the selected institutions onto a Cartesian coordinate system, where δ is placed on the x-axis and ρ on the y-axis. The **origin** of the axes is defined by the average values of δ (6) and ρ (5). The four regions generated by the axes create a 2×2 matrix, which we will refer to as the **Institutional Positioning Matrix** (see Figure 5.2). Actors are represented as circles, with a diameter corresponding to their γ value. The **fill color** indicates their classification: Black for *Strategic Actors*, Dark Gray for *Enablers*, Light Gray for *Commercial Actors*, and White for *Balanced Actors*.

Let us now focus on the individual quadrants of the matrix. It is important to note that actors within the same quadrant may still be in very different situations. For example, consider a subject positioned at the upper extreme of the *Complex Criticality* quadrant (value 12;9): although it shares the same quadrant with another actor at (7;6), its situation is significantly more difficult.

5.2.1   Understanding the Meaning of Each Quadrant and the Corresponding Strategic Guidelines

- **Complex Criticality.** This represents the most challenging situation: the public entity is characterized by significant internal difficulties, and the

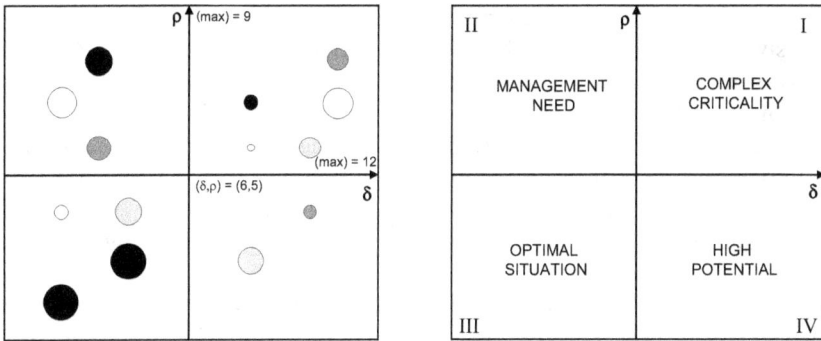

Figure 5.2 Institutional positioning matrix.

Legend

δ: Relationship Difficulty x-axis   Black: Strategic Actors
ρ: Relational Risk y-axis   Dark gray: Enablers
γ: Relationship Importance circle   Light gray: Commercial Actors
diameter   White: Balanced Actors

relationship with the company is consequently problematic. A PA intervention with these institutions is justifiable only when they show high levels of relevance (b, t, γ), as the chances of success are limited and require substantial investment to achieve any meaningful result.

- **Management Need.** Here, we are dealing with institutions that do not present internal issues but tend to collaborate more with competing companies than with ours. This is a situation where PA intervention is both urgent and necessary, as we are effectively losing opportunities to the benefit of competitors. This strategic indication must then be complemented by operational considerations – in terms of planning and timing – to define appropriate modes of intervention.

- **High Potential.** These are institutions with which we have a favorable relationship, but internal complexities prevent us from fully capitalizing on it. The low relational risk facilitates engagement, and it is possible that a niche may emerge where an effective initiative can be developed. These actors must be carefully monitored, as our favorable positioning should enable us to promptly seize any opportunity that arises when the institution resumes full functionality.

- **Optimal Situation.** This is the quadrant where we would ideally like to place most of our institutional counterparts. Here, difficulties are minimal, and the risk of a relational crisis is low. Such situations can be managed without the need for specific interventions; in fact, it is advisable to maintain the current management approach. All key public stakeholders for a company should, ideally, fall into this category.

Once stakeholders are positioned within the matrix, we obtain a comprehensive yet detailed view of the institutional landscape. This serves not only as a strategic overview but also as a **powerful organizational coordination tool**, supporting alignment with other business functions. It facilitates the prioritization of actions, scheduling and **measurement of PA outcomes** (as we will see in Section 6.4).

The situation captured in the matrix naturally evolves over time – both as a result of external developments and through our own actions. For this reason, the analysis should be repeated periodically (on average, every six months) to track changes. The use of **AI can be particularly valuable** in two ways: first, to help identify possible interventions aimed at improving the variables shown in the matrix; and second, simulate, through reverse modeling, the potential impact of planned initiatives on the values represented in the framework.

Having mapped individual institutions and defined tailored strategies for each, we can now elevate our perspective to consider how these relationships collectively shape the company's overall institutional positioning. This brings us to the corporate-level strategy, where high-level guidelines align Public Affairs efforts with broader business objectives.

5.2.2   Institutional Corporate Strategy

We now shift from the operational strategy concerning individual institutions to a corporate-level strategy, in which we define the **company's strategic guidelines toward the overall public landscape**.

We construct a single indicator representing the company's institutional positioning, based on the individual situations illustrated in Figure 5.2. This allows us to obtain a simple, high-level overview that supports strategic reflection and decision-making at the corporate level.

To build this indicator, we calculate a **weighted average of the risk levels** ρ and difficulties δ, where the weights are determined by the subject's technical and commercial impact (see Figure 5.1).

The weighting system is as follows:

Strategic Actors → weight = 3

Commercial Actors and *Enablers* → weight = 2

Balanced Actors → weight = 1

We also compute an average γ, using a simple arithmetic mean of the individual values.

Let (n) be the number of stakeholders considered, and w_i the weight assigned to each actor based on its classification:

Weighted Risk Index $(\bar{\rho})$:

$$\bar{\rho} = \left(\Sigma\, w_i \cdot \rho_i\right) / \left(\Sigma\, w_i\right)$$

Weighted Difficulty Index $(\bar{\delta})$:

$$\bar{\delta} = \left(\Sigma\, w_i \cdot \delta_i\right) / \left(\Sigma\, w_i\right)$$

Average Importance $(\bar{\gamma})$:

$$\bar{\gamma} = \left(\Sigma\, \gamma_i\right) / n$$

At this point, we can **position the representative circle of the company's overall institutional positioning** on the usual coordinate system (δ, ρ); the diameter of the circle corresponds to the average γ previously calculated.

To understand whether the institutional relationships maintained by the company are meaningful within its operating context, we must **compare the number of managed relationships to the total number of relevant public actors**. Indeed, importance γ qualifies the relational network, but it is not directly correlated with the number of stakeholders being actively managed. The number of institutions to be managed has no absolute benchmark, and it does not necessarily grow over time. It depends on the total number of relevant public stakeholders in the specific sector or territory, and, secondarily, on the company's strategic choices.

Starting from the total number of relevant stakeholders (N), we now compare this value with the **number (q) for which we actively carry out PA interventions**. The institutions to be counted under (q) are those for which at least one of the core PA processes (see Figure 1.2) is underway.

Generally, (q) coincides with the number of actors (n) included in the Matrix shown in Figure 5.2 and used to calculate the average values of (δ, ρ, γ). However, there may be cases in which, for example, actions toward certain stakeholders are planned but not yet implemented. In that case, the actor cannot be considered as "managed," and we would have $q < n$.

We define the following rule to represent this comparison – the percentage of institutions actively managed at the PA level compared to the total number of relevant public actors – as follows:

- If $q > 75\%$ of N, we are in an optimal situation → *black color.*
- If 50% of $N < q \leq 75\%$ of N, we are in a good situation → *dark gray color.*

- If 25% of N < q ≤ 50% of N, we are in a somewhat acceptable situation → *light gray color*.
- If q ≤ 25% of N, we are in an unacceptable situation → *white color*.

Figure 5.3 shows an example of a Corporate Institutional Positioning Matrix.

It now becomes possible to define a **Corporate Strategic Objective** that will guide the operational strategies toward individual institutions. Naturally, this strategic choice must align with the company's medium- to long-term goals, which, to be effectively pursued, require a coherent PA strategy.

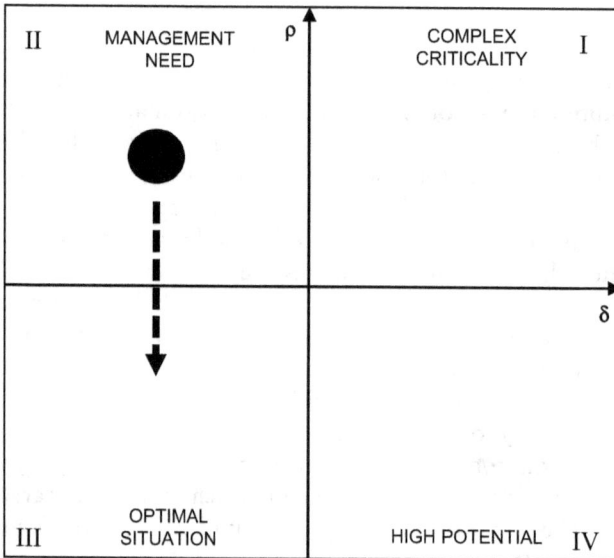

Legend

δ: Relationship Difficulty x-axis	Black: q>75%N
ρ: Relational Risk y-axis	Dark gray: 50%N<q<75%N
γ: Relationship Importance – circle diameter	Light gray: 25%N<q<50%N
	White: q<25%N
	N: Number of Relevant Institutions
	q: Number of Institutions Being Managed

Figure 5.3 Corporate institutional positioning matrix.

At the level of *Corporate Institutional Strategy*, **three main objectives** can be identified:

1. **Strengthening Relationships.** The company makes a deliberate decision to invest in institutional engagement, either by reinforcing existing relationships or by developing new ones. This approach may be driven by various factors, most commonly as a response to a corporate need to advance a project requiring adequate institutional support. In other instances, this strategy may be adopted to address a current positioning that fails to meet evolving business needs or to initiate collaboration with new public stakeholders.
2. **Managing Relationships.** This option may result from satisfaction with the current institutional positioning. It typically reflects the situation of a mature company with a well-established PA framework. Nonetheless, this objective is not cost-neutral: maintaining and consolidating relationships still demands organizational energy and attention.
3. **Concentrating or Reducing Relationships.** This choice may stem from various conditions and, contrary to common assumptions, does not always indicate a negative trend in institutional relations. While deliberately ending a productive and strategic relationship is generally inadvisable, scaling back efforts to initiate new connections can be a sound strategic move, especially when such connections fail to generate value or meaningful prospects. In all cases, optimization may be achieved by pruning inactive or unproductive relationships, provided they do not hold strategic relevance for the company.

Table 5.4 summarizes the three corporate-level strategic objectives and the **expected variations in the average values of key relational variables.** It is important to note that the PA function can act upon variables q (quantity) and p (risk), whereas γ (importance) tends to remain stable over the medium-to-long term, and changes in δ (difficulty) are largely beyond the

Table 5.4 Corporate Strategic Relational Objectives

	Number of Relationships (q_m)	Difficulty δ_m	Relational Risk ρ_m	Importance γ_m
Strengthening	Stable or increasing	Variable	Marked decrease	Marginal improvement
Management	Stable	No significant change	Marginal decrease	No significant change
Reduction	Progressive reduction	Variable	Variable	Marked increase

company's control. However, whenever actors are added to or removed from the corporate stakeholder matrix, shifts may occur in the average values of γ and δ as well.

5.3   Building an Effective Digital Strategy

In the previous section, we discussed how to define a PA strategy. We now turn to the development of a DPA strategy that aligns with it, while taking into account the specific digital behaviors of the public institutions under consideration.

We begin with the *Institutional Positioning Matrix* (Figure 5.2), from which we immediately derive the public actors to prioritize. The variables used in this phase are as follows:

- **Relational Value on Relationship Importance** (m / γ): this variable considers exclusively the business and technical impact of the institution on the company, disregarding its institutional relevance (see Section 5.1). It does not have a predefined value range and will be represented graphically using a proportionally scaled visual indicator.
- **Relational Risk** ρ: this variable ranges from 0 to 9 (see Section 3.4).
- **WSM Propensity** π: this new variable expresses the tendency of a public actor to maintain a presence on WSM channels. To determine π, we calculate the average number of posts published by each institution of interest over a given time frame (typically one year). A scale from 0 to 9 is then defined, ranging from no posts to the highest level of activity. AI tools can support the tracking and computation of these values.

We then map the identified actors on a Cartesian coordinate system based on the variables above. *WSM Propensity* π is plotted on the x-axis and *Relational Risk* ρ on the y-axis. The origin is set at coordinates (5, 5). This leads us to construct the first **Institutional Digital Positioning Matrix** (see Figure 5.4), a 2×2 matrix in which each public actor is represented by a circle. The radius of each circle corresponds to the value of (m / γ), while the fill pattern is used solely to distinguish one actor from another.

Let us now explore the meaning of the four quadrants in the first matrix, bearing in mind that within each quadrant there are behavioral nuances based on the specific values of the variables:

- (π): **low** – (ρ): **low** → **Silent Ally**. This scenario is characterized by a stable and unproblematic relationship, with no significant short-term risks. Furthermore, the institution rarely uses digital channels. As such, we do not anticipate online threats from this actor. On the contrary, given the strength of the relationship, we might even consider asking them to publicly voice support for our position, leveraging what can

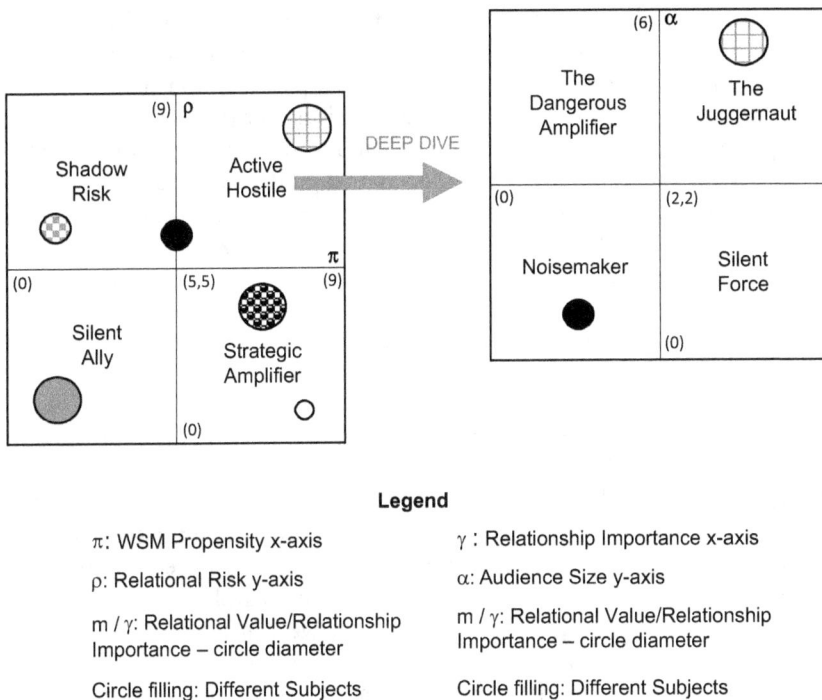

Figure 5.4 Institutional digital positioning matrix.

become a strategic asset. A WSM appearance from an entity that rarely uses such platforms is often more impactful than posts by habitual users of these channels.

- (π): **low** – (ρ): **high** → **Shadow Risk.** In this quadrant, the actors are largely absent from the WSM landscape and do not maintain a favorable relationship with the company. In this case, the lack of digital activity works to our advantage and should not be encouraged. The appropriate course of action is to rely on traditional PA efforts, aiming to reduce *Relational Risk* (see Section 3.4), especially when anticipating potentially critical developments. This situation is the symmetrical opposite of the *Silent Ally* quadrant: it represents a latent threat, a sort of sword of Damocles that may fall due to either direct institutional actions or advocacy efforts triggered by third parties.

- (π): **high** – (ρ): **low** → **Strategic Amplifier.** This is the most favorable scenario: the institution is active on WSM channels and enjoys a positive relationship with the company. This positioning may be the result of an ongoing engagement, whether already visible in digital support or yet to materialize. In either case, it offers a strong opportunity both for direct communication and for integrating the actor into a broader advocacy initiative, potentially assigning them a partnership role.

- (π): high – (ρ): high → **Active Hostile**. This is a critical situation. When a public actor is highly active on WSM and maintains a poor relationship with the company, the associated digital risk is substantial and requires careful management. This scenario is examined in further detail in the second *Institutional Digital Positioning Matrix*, indicated by the arrow in Figure 5.4.

To explore this final scenario in greater depth, we will use the following variables:

- **Institutional Relationship Importance** (γ): this variable ranges from 0 to 6 (see Section 5.1).
- **Audience Size** (α): this attribute refers to the number of followers that the actor – either directly or indirectly (e.g., through affiliated influencers) – is capable of mobilizing around a specific topic (see Section 4.2). Standard metrics from social media marketing can be used to measure this indicator. For the sake of simplicity, we can refer to the average number of followers of the relevant public institutions and construct a scale from 0 to 6 based on proportional follower counts. More sophisticated versions of this variable could also account for the impact of the institution's WSM activity, the authority of its followers, or the influence of those who engage with its posts.

We then place these variables on a Cartesian coordinate system, with γ on the x-axis and α on the y-axis. The origin is set at (2,2), as values above 2 for both variables already indicate a certain level of significance. The circles used in this second matrix are the same as those carried over from the first matrix, representing the actors under further analysis.

Let us now examine the **strategic implications** of positioning an institutional actor within each of the quadrants:

- (γ): low – (α): low → **Noisemaker**. This type of actor may be hostile and active on WSM, but they lack both a substantial following and institutional relevance. In such cases, it is generally unwise to initiate or escalate public disputes, as doing so may grant them undue visibility and create unnecessary complications. However, if necessary, a well-calibrated counteraction can be considered. Respect for institutions remains fundamental, but it must not evolve into a reverential fear that prevents the organization from firmly asserting its stance.
- (γ): low – (α): high → **The Dangerous Amplifier**. In this case, the institution does not maintain a positive relationship with the company, yet it

possesses significant digital reach and the ability to aggregate attention through WSM. This makes the situation particularly delicate. While their institutional influence γ may be limited, even a score of (2) warrants caution. These actors typically have a strong communication focus. Digital and institutional interactions should therefore be managed separately. When it comes to online responses, it is often best to rely on professional communicators – such as *Star influencers* (see Section 4.3) – who have the tools and networks necessary to contain and counter digital messaging effectively.

- (γ): **high** – (α): **low** → **Silent Force.** These actors are politically relevant and they also tend to use WSM channels, though not with exceptional results. Despite their limited digital footprint, their institutional weight makes them actors that require careful handling. Engaging in public online debate with such stakeholders is not advisable. Doing so risks inadvertently amplifying their visibility and legitimizing their position, even if they are not highly active online.

- (γ): **high** – (α): **high** → **The Juggernaut.** This is the most challenging scenario. The institution is both influential and highly capable in digital communication. In such cases, any DPA initiative must be part of an exceptionally well-crafted PA and DPA strategy. The company must be prepared to launch a full-scale digital engagement, mobilizing influencers and other credible stakeholders to design and execute an effective advocacy campaign that strengthens its position. One must be aware of and ready to manage the significant relational risk involved in confronting such an institution.

Here too, the double verification of the actor's position using different pairs of variables serves both to reinforce the assessment and to provide strategic guidance on how to act.

Once the *Institutional Digital Positioning Matrices* are completed, they offer a **comprehensive overview of the company's institutional relationships in the digital sphere.** They also provide **strategic guidance** on how to approach each actor, guidance that is invaluable for the design of **advocacy initiatives** (see Sections 3.5 and 5.4). When read in conjunction with the *Institutional Positioning Matrix* (see Figure 5.2), they enable the development of an **integrated and coherent PA and DPA strategy.**

5.4 Reverse Advocacy

Before moving on to the final section, where the overall *Public Affairs Management* model is outlined, we shall mention *Reverse Advocacy* as a strategic tool to support institutional communication activities.

Reverse Advocacy refers to a strategic dynamic in which **public institutions exert influence on companies,** industry groups, or civil society stakeholders to prompt behavioral changes or to garner support for specific policies. Unlike traditional advocacy – where private actors seek to influence public decision-makers – *Reverse Advocacy* involves public sector entities actively promoting private initiatives.

To better understand the mechanics of *Reverse Advocacy*, consider the case of a company launching a major project capable of generating local wealth, creating jobs, or expanding access to services. While the company may require certain incentives or regulatory facilitations, it simultaneously offers the institution the opportunity to act as a partner in the initiative by **publicly endorsing** and supporting it. As a result, the public institution is perceived by beneficiaries (citizens, businesses, etc.) as a co-implementer of the project, thereby enhancing its public image and increasing its political consensus. Figure 5.4 compares *Advocacy* and *Reverse Advocacy*.

In essence, the **company shares a politically communicable opportunity with the institution,** one that brings tangible benefits to the affected population and, in turn, builds consensus around the public entity that promotes it. In practical terms, the political actor is handed a cost-free opportunity "on a silver platter." The policymaker can then amplify the company's initiative through appropriate communication channels, including, naturally, all digital and online media.

Figure 5.5 compares the typical processes of Advocacy and Reverse Advocacy.

This process typically **involves multiple actors,** depending both on the dynamics that gave rise to the initiative and on the opportunities identified by the company and the institutions. In Table 5.5, we identify the **predominant interests of the main actors** generally involved in this process. Both rows and columns list the same actors; the subject in the row is the requester and the subject in the column is the recipient of the request. What emerges is the need for cross-collaboration to ensure that the positive outcomes of

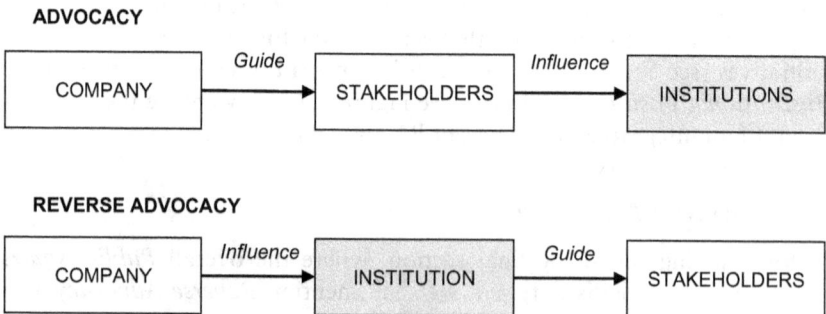

ADVOCACY

REVERSE ADVOCACY

Figure 5.5 Advocacy and reverse advocacy.

Table 5.5 Reverse Advocacy: Stakeholder Relationships

	Institution	Intermediaries	Beneficiary	Our Company
Institution		Collaboration and support	Consensus	Collaboration and development
Intermediaries	Collaboration and involvement		Involvement	Long-lasting and transparent dialogue
Beneficiary	Guarantees of implementation and transparency	Support over time when needed		Access to benefits
Our Company	Promotion and/or facilitation	Collaboration	Membership or other relevant forms	

the initiative are shared. The owner of the initiative holds a position of strength and should therefore aim to maximize both relational and communication returns.

The most suitable communication methods for promoting the activities shown in the corresponding cells are, naturally, those of traditional communication and WSM, except in cases of dialogue between institutions and companies or intermediaries, where a behind-closed-doors negotiation process (i.e., private meetings) is typically assumed.

5.5   Public Affairs Management – Strategic Model

The traditional image of the lobbyist engaging in persuasive dialogue with the policymaker belongs to the past. The practice of Public Affairs has evolved into a complex, multi-dimensional puzzle of relationships, content, data-driven analysis, and advocacy strategies, enhanced and amplified by artificial intelligence.

This is the final section dedicated to external-facing PA activities. Up to this point, we have explored the strategic, operational, and analytical dimensions, as well as the use of digital technologies applied for this purpose. The next chapter will focus on internal organizational aspects, including structure, skills, resources, and related topics.

We will now present an **integrated view of the company's overall PA strategic model**, bringing together the elements discussed so far and capturing a reality that is constantly evolving. This evolution pushes organizations to integrate innovative tools into traditional relational methodologies, with the goal of leveraging every possible avenue to achieve their objectives.

All the PA activities and tools described thus far can be categorized into three classes (each associated with a specific color code which will be used in Figure 5.6). Within these classes, we will outline the **types of activities** that characterize them:

- **Strategic** (Light Gray): activities focused on defining PA strategies and managing high-level relationships with key stakeholders and policymakers. These actions require negotiation, advocacy, and complex decision-making, where AI can support by providing intelligence, scenario analysis, and stakeholder mapping, but the human relational component remains central and irreplaceable.

    1. *Strategic Institutional Engagement.* High-level engagement with key public institutions to build, consolidate, and strengthen the company's long-term positioning and influence within institutional ecosystems.

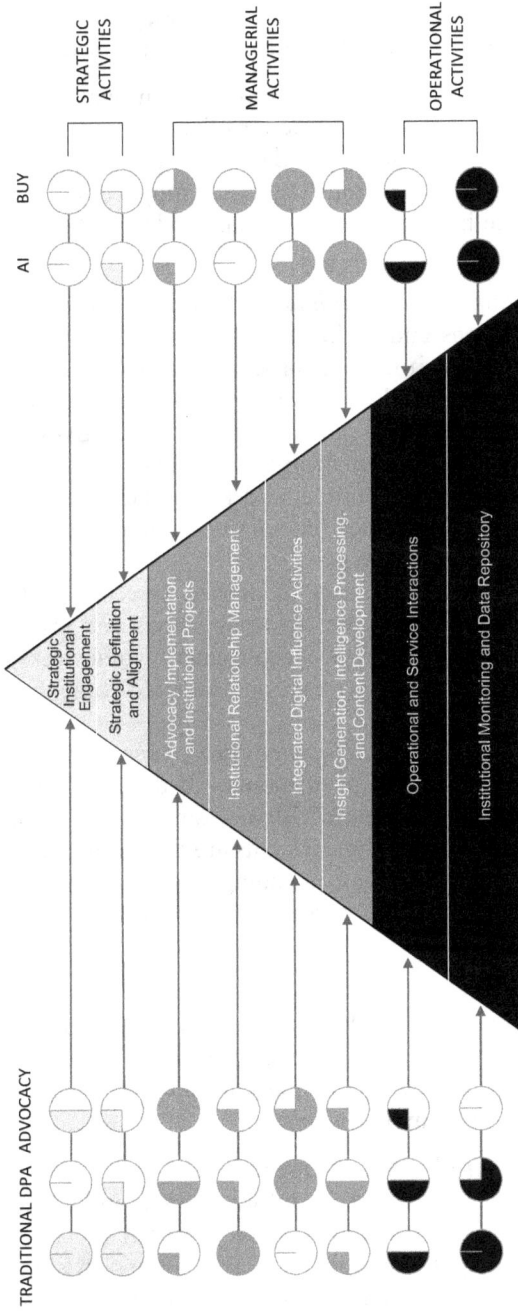

Figure 5.6 Public affairs management – Strategic model.

2. *Strategic Definition and Alignment.* Definition of PA strategic priorities and alignment with corporate objectives, providing the framework that guides all institutional engagement and advocacy activities.

- **Managerial** (Dark Gray): Activities that operationalize strategic guidelines into specific PA plans and actions, balancing traditional relationship-building with the use of digital tools (DPA). AI can assist in content personalization, issue monitoring, and supporting decision-making processes, while human oversight ensures adaptability and contextual relevance.

3. *Advocacy Implementation and Institutional Projects.* Execution of advocacy actions and realization of institutional projects aimed at influencing decision-making processes; supporting strategic objectives; and mobilizing key stakeholders through high-level meetings, events, partnerships and public positioning initiatives.

4. *Institutional Relationship Management.* Day-to-day management of relationships with institutions and key stakeholders, ensuring continuous engagement, timely interactions, and responsiveness to institutional needs and requests.

5. *Integrated Digital Influence Activities.* Execution of coordinated digital activities to support advocacy efforts and institutional positioning. This includes WSM engagement, influencer partnerships, online reputation management, and targeted content dissemination across digital platforms.

6. *Insight Generation, Intelligence Processing, and Content Development.* Transformation of monitored data and institutional signals into actionable insights, risk assessments, and scenario analyses to guide PA priorities. These insights are then translated into strategic content and key messages, including position papers, policy briefs, advocacy materials, and narrative frameworks designed to support institutional engagement and advocacy efforts.

- **Operational** (Black): routine activities supporting PA execution, such as monitoring, reporting, and dissemination of standardized content. These are highly automatable processes where AI plays a primary role in automating workflows, data analysis, and content generation, with limited need for human intervention.

7. *Operational and Service Interactions.* Operational interactions aimed at providing technical, informational, and service support to both public institutions and internal company functions involved in PA activities. These activities may include the provision of corporate data, operational updates, technical briefings, and institutional

briefings, as well as supporting internal teams with information and tools needed to enable advocacy efforts, stakeholder engagement, or institutional dialogue.

8. *Institutional Monitoring and Data Repository.* Systematic collection of institutional, political, regulatory, economic, and reputational data. Includes legislative acts, policy proposals, public statements, stakeholder positions, media reports, and social signals. Creation of an organized data repository as a foundational knowledge base.

The three classes (*Strategic, Managerial, Operational*) are characterized by different levels of effort, with operational activities requiring the most significant effort and strategic activities the least. However, strategic activities are distinguished by their higher added value. In Figure 5.6, this difference is visually represented by the **width of the triangles' bases**, where the *Dark Gray* triangles (*Operational*) are noticeably larger, indicating a greater effort.

In addition to the main triangular model, Figure 5.6 also includes pie charts using a five-level scale (ranging from null to four quarters). The **pie charts on the left illustrate the relevance of Traditional Institutional Relations, Digital (DPA)**, and **Advocacy** for each of the eight identified activities. Conversely, the pie charts on the right depict the contribution that **AI** can provide to each activity, as well as the potential for outsourcing within a **Make or Buy** perspective.

It is worth noting that the **Public Affairs Management model does not explicitly feature lobbying as a standalone activity.** From a managerial perspective, lobbying is spread across multiple activities. In its most traditional sense, lobbying can be clearly identified within Institutional Monitoring, in the analysis and Content Development processes, and in Relationship Activities.

Bibliography

Di Giacomo G., *Institutional Marketing & Public Affairs: Managing Institutional Relations to Create Value for the Business*, Franco Angeli Editore, Milan (IT), 2019.

Gelak D., *Lobbying and Advocacy: Winning Strategies, Resources, Recommendations, Ethics and Ongoing Compliance for Lobbyists and Washington Advocates*, TheCapitol.Net, Inc., Alexandria VA, 2008.

Johnson G., Scholes K., Whittington R., *Exploring Corporate Strategy: Text and Cases*, Pearson Education Limited, London (UK), 2008.

Libby P., *The Lobbying Strategy Handbook: 10 Steps to Advancing Any Cause Effectively*, Oxford University Press, Oxford (UK), 2020.

Porter M., *Competitive Strategy: Techniques for Analyzing Industries and Competitors*, Free Press, 2008. https://www.amazon.it/Competitive-Strategy-Techniques-Industries-Competitors-ebook/dp/B001CB34J0/ref=tmm_kin_swatch_0#detailBullets_feature_div

Stern C.W., Deimler M.S., *The Boston Consulting Group on Strategy: Classic Concepts and New Perspectives*, Wiley, New York, 2007.

Chapter 6

Organizing Tools

6.1 Structure and Operations of the Public Affairs Function

This chapter is entirely dedicated to the structure and management of a PA function. It addresses key aspects such as organizational design, internal processes, required competencies, budget allocation, and performance measurement.

The organizational architecture of a PA function can be developed through different models. In this section, we will highlight the specific characteristics required for this function, beginning with the definition of the **typical roles** and **core responsibilities**:

- **Chief Public Affairs Officer:** the top executive who leads the function, ensuring strategic guidance and high-level representation. The role may be supported by a PMO or deputy director to coordinate operations.
- **Institutional Relations Units:** these units are responsible for managing relationships with external stakeholders. Activities are typically segmented – most commonly – by geographical area, but may also be organized by policy domain or stakeholder category (e.g., institutions, trade associations, subject-matter experts, etc.).
- **Advocacy and DPA Unit:** this unit is in charge of advocacy initiatives, the management of institutional projects, and the development of DPA strategies.
- **Leadership Affairs Office:** this unit supports top management in all institutional matters. Its primary responsibilities include the production of strategic content and the coordination of public relations activities.

The *Relationship Management Functions*, operating in alignment with the strategic guidelines set by the *Chief Public Affairs Officer*, independently oversee engagement with institutional stakeholders within their respective domains. These units work in close coordination to ensure seamless integration across international, national, and local levels when required.

DOI: 10.4324/9781003647829-7

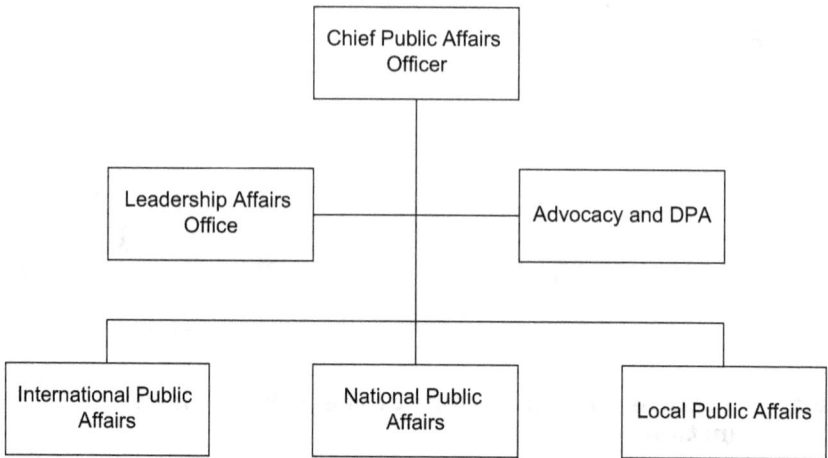

Figure 6.1 Public affairs function organizational structure.

They also maintain ongoing collaboration with the two Staff Units, which act both as **internal centers of excellence** and as catalysts for advocacy initiatives.

This structure underlines the **need for constant alignment** among all involved actors to ensure that operational strategies and programs are properly implemented and that any changes prompted by the external context are promptly shared and addressed.

Figure 6.1 illustrates a typical organizational chart of a PA function, where institutional relationships are segmented on a territorial basis.

Box 6.1 examines the main positioning options for a PA function within the corporate organizational chart.

Box 6.1   The Organizational Placement of the Public Affairs function

The PA function is sometimes positioned within a broader corporate area. This configuration often reflects specific organizational needs or a relatively low strategic relevance of institutions to the core business. The most common cases **place the PA function** within the following structures:

- **Chief External Relations Office.** Grouped with Communication and often ESG (Environmental, Social, and Governance), with the aim of fostering alignment and synergies in stakeholder engagement and external messaging.

- **Chief Regulatory/Legal Affairs Office.** Combined with Legal and/ or Regulatory Affairs units – particularly in countries with regulated markets overseen by independent authorities – especially when the PA function focuses on lobbying and the coordination of legislative proposals is a strategic priority.
- **Chief Corporate Affairs Office.** In this case, PA is embedded within a corporate staff function that may also oversee areas such as Human Resources, Strategy, and Procurement, in addition to the domains mentioned above.

Regardless of the structural arrangement adopted, the considerations discussed in terms of organization, roles, and activities remain fully applicable.

For each of the roles presented, Table 6.1 outlines the typical activities carried out both within the function/company and externally. For clarity, DPA and Advocacy activities are presented separately, although they are part of the same unit. Finally, with regard to DPA, it should be noted that externally oriented activities are, by their very nature, conducted through digital channels.

Table 6.1 Key Activities by Role within the Public Affairs Function

Role	External Activities	Internal Activities
Chief Public Affairs Officer	– Manages relationships with senior institutional figures and intermediaries – Represents the company at key events and high-level working sessions – Personally handles particularly sensitive or strategic cases – Accompanies top executives to major institutional meetings	– Defines the overall PA strategy and key initiatives – Establishes the company's official positions on institutional issues – Maintains direct liaison with top management – Interfaces with other functions to integrate PA into strategic planning and coordination – Manages human resources within the PA function – Approves the department's budget

(Continued)

Table 6.1 (Continued)

Role	External Activities	Internal Activities
Institutional Relations Units	– Manages relationships with institutions (see Figures 2.1, 3.1, 3.2) – Represents the company in institutional settings and working groups – Implements PA tools and techniques in the field (see Tables 3.3 and 3.6) – Collaborates on Advocacy projects	– Drafts and updates strategic institutional reports (see Figures 2.1, 2.3, 2.5 and Tables 5.1, 5.3) – Provides institutional intelligence to internal PA units – Supports business units on public-sector-related matters – Monitors legislative and regulatory developments
Advocacy Unit	– Manages Advocacy projects autonomously or jointly with Institutional Relations Units – Builds early-stage alliances with external stakeholders	– Designs Advocacy initiatives (see Table 3.14) – Develops content for PA technical tools (see Table 3.3) – Promotes Reverse Advocacy opportunities (see Figure 5.5) – Acts as PMO for Advocacy initiatives
DPA Unit	– Manages online DPA activities and related discussions on WSM (see Tables 4.1, 4.2, 4.5, 4.6) – Implements digital components of Advocacy projects	– Analyzes stakeholders' digital positioning (see Figure 2.4) – Develops digital strategies (see Tables 4.3, 4.4, 4.9) – Collaborates with corporate functions managing digital presence – Selects influencers (see Figure 4.1)
Leadership Affairs Office	– Supports the CEO/President in institutional engagements (see Table 3.6) – Coordinates the institutional presence of the corporate leadership	– Contributes to the development of PA Technical Tools (see Table 3.3), particularly in economic, political, social, and sectoral analysis – Aligns leadership positioning with PA priorities – Prepares talking points and executive briefings

(Continued)

Table 6.1 (Continued)

Role	External Activities	Internal Activities
Chief PMO	– Provides support during institutional and advocacy engagements	– Updates strategic documents such as the Impact Map of Public Stakeholders (Figure 5.1), Corporate/Institutional Positioning Matrix (Figures 5.2, 5.3), and Institutional Relational Development Potential (Figure 2.6) – Prepares and monitors the PA function's budget – Oversees project timelines, functional activities (Figures 2.7, 2.8, 2.9), and performance – Gathers and shares data and requests across corporate departments

Once the core responsibilities of each unit have been defined, we complete the framework by outlining their **main interactions**. Table 6.2 highlights the most significant activities each role requests from the other organizational units. The actors listed in the rows initiate the requests, while the units in the columns are the recipients.

It is worth briefly emphasizing the **matrix-based structure of the model**: the units responsible for producing projects and content (*Advocacy Unit, Leadership Affairs Office*) serve and support the relational frontlines – both traditional (*Institutional Relationship Units*) and digital (*DPA Unit*) – while also receiving essential feedback that ensures the constant alignment of initiatives with evolving institutional dynamics.

Another key element is the **close and continuous collaboration among the relational frontlines**, which enables the rapid coordination of initiatives – even short-term ones – by leveraging all available channels. Strategic and operational **governance** of the PA function lies, respectively, with the *Chief* and the PMO, who also facilitate information flow and ensure both short- and long-term coordination.

Table 6.2 Internal Interactions across PA Units

From\To	Chief	PMO	Institutional Relationship Units	Advocacy Unit	DPA Unit	Leadership Affairs Office
Chief		Requests reporting and risk monitoring	Provides strategic direction and objectives. Coordinates critical initiatives	Approves Advocacy projects	Provides general and specific guidelines (see Table 4.9)	Forwards top management requests and commissions analyses
PMO	Provides function activities reports		Ensures vertical coordination among units	Monitors project progress and facilitates knowledge sharing	Collects information and supports WSM-related decisions	Ensures institutional engagement planning and the reporting of PA milestones to top management
Institutional Relationship Units	Share activities and request support for external/internal actions	Provide data and updates on institutional relations		Collaborate in a value chain perspective	Request DPA actions in support of traditional initiatives	Use analytical outputs and provide feedback

From\To	Chief	PMO	Institutional Relationship Units	Advocacy Unit	DPA Unit	Leadership Affairs Office
Advocacy Unit	Propose projects and plan stakeholder engagement	Provide data and updates on Advocacy initiatives	Propose and co-develop initiatives		Share DPA-related needs within projects	Flag relevant activities and request analytical support
DPA Unit	Share relevant WSM-related choices	Provide integrated reports on WSM activities	Propose and implement digital activities aligned with traditional efforts	Ensure WSM coverage and provide feedback		Verify alignment of WSM content with top management messaging
Leadership Affairs Office	Request approval of content intended for top management	Share institutional activities of leadership	Receive updates	Collaborate on content creation and refinement	Request digital-based analyses	

The following Box 6.2 highlights the need to enable the PA function to operate effectively by ensuring its full understanding of the company's strategic and operational processes, which may have both direct and indirect impacts on institutions.

Box 6.2   Organizational Integration Mechanisms for Public Affairs

A necessary condition for the PA function to create value for the company is its **full integration into corporate processes**. Only through this alignment can institutional relationships be managed effectively and the tools discussed in previous chapters be continuously nourished and activated. This integration must occur at multiple levels and is supported by **formalized organizational mechanisms**, as outlined below:

- **Top Executive Level.** This refers exclusively to the *Chief Public Affairs Officer*, who represents the function at the highest levels of the company.

  - *Direct Reporting*: the Chief reports directly to the CEO or a member of the Executive Committee, ensuring strategic alignment and visibility.
  - *Top Management Committee*: participation in high-level management committees allows for the proactive management of institutional dimensions within corporate decision-making processes.

- **Managerial Level.** This includes the heads of the various PA units, who are responsible for implementing strategy.

  - *Cross-functional Coordination Group*: a structured platform that enables regular interaction with other key corporate functions, facilitating alignment on institutional priorities and consistency in initiatives.
- **Operational Level.** This involves all PA professionals engaged in the daily execution of activities.

  - *Working Groups*: ad hoc teams set up to address specific dossiers or projects, often involving joint participation from other business areas.
  - *Digital Collaboration Tools*: corporate platforms (e.g., intranet, shared drives, project management tools) that ensure timely sharing of information, documents, and updates on institutional relationships.

6.2   Staffing the Public Affairs Function

We now turn to the identification of professional profiles required to staff the PA function, along with the sizing of its organizational units (Figure 6.1). The first critical issue we encounter is the absence of a universally accepted definition of the PA professional. Unlike more consolidated functions – such as marketing or finance – **Public Affairs lacks a standardized professional profile** and remains an emerging discipline within management literature. As a result, companies must independently identify the most appropriate profiles, selecting individuals whose skills and training align with the specific demands of the role they are expected to perform within the function.

The ideal PA professional is required to master a wide-ranging and interdisciplinary set of competencies. These span political and institutional knowledge, legal and economic literacy, communication capabilities, digital proficiency, and, crucially, deep expertise in the sector in which the company operates. Complementing these **technical skills** is a robust set of **soft skills**, particularly those geared toward relationship-building, collaboration, and negotiation. Unsurprisingly, such a profile is rarely available on the job market "as is," but must instead be shaped over time, through a dynamic and continuous learning process in which the company plays a central role.

Moreover, the pace at which the field evolves – driven by regulatory change, technological innovation (e.g., artificial intelligence), and frequent cross-sector mobility – makes the development of PA talent an inherently fluid and strategic endeavor.

Table 6.3 outlines the technical competencies and soft skills required for professionals working within the various organizational units of the PA function. The final column lists the analytical variables used to help determine the **ideal number of staff members for each unit.**

Table 6.3 Technical Competencies, Soft Skills, and Key Sizing Variables

Role	Technical Competencies	Soft Skills	Key Sizing Variables
Chief Public Affairs Officer	Strategic management; Project ideation and design; Policy-making processes; Sector-specific expertise; Multilingual proficiency; Human resources and budget management.	Political judgment; Executive presence; Decision-making under uncertainty; Influence and negotiation; Strategic interpersonal communication.	-

(Continued)

Table 6.3 (Continued)

Role	Technical Competencies	Soft Skills	Key Sizing Variables
Institutional Relations Units	Political science and public administration; Business and organizational management; Legal and regulatory frameworks; Institutional communication; Industry knowledge.	Relationship management; Political sensitivity; Stakeholder empathy and active listening; Negotiation; Teamwork and collaboration.	Geographic presence; Relevance and scope of organizational mandate; Number of stakeholders; Company lifecycle phase; Regulatory and legislative pressure.
Advocacy Unit	Advocacy and institutional marketing; Public communication; Cost-benefit and cost-effectiveness analysis; Project structuring and execution.	Strategic thinking; Communication clarity and knowledge sharing; Teamwork and collaboration; Persuasion.	Project complexity (number, stakeholder density, implementation difficulty, geographic spread, multi-channel strategy); Budget and resource availability; Outcome-driven pressure.
Digital Public Affairs Unit	Digital engagement strategy; Data analytics and stakeholder tools; Media relations and crisis management; Use of AI platforms and monitoring tools.	Analytical thinking; Situational awareness; Creativity; Adaptability; Strategic communication; Technological affinity.	IT platform operation level; Number of variables (actors, issues, projects); Required responsiveness and time coverage; Degree of autonomy; Strategic relevance of DPA.
Leadership Affairs Office	Socio-economic and political context analysis; Legal and regulatory competence; Institutional speechwriting; Thought leadership development.	Research and analytical thinking; Discretion; Synthesis and clarity; High-level relational style; Stress resilience.	Level of support to top executives; Frequency and intensity of executive engagement; Content volume and sensitivity; Strategic weight of leadership support activities.

(Continued)

Table 6.3 (Continued)

Role	Technical Competencies	Soft Skills	Key Sizing Variables
Chief PMO	Workflow and project planning; KPI monitoring and evaluation; Strategic and executive reporting; Budget planning and financial oversight.	Precision; Process orientation; Problem solving; Internal coordination.	Overall project load; Coordination complexity across units; Level of delegation and operational autonomy.

The actual staffing of a PA function can vary significantly depending on the size of the company, the markets in which it operates, the number of countries involved, and the breadth of its organizational mandate. As a result, PA teams can range in size from as few as 2 to over 50 professionals. For each PA role, the typical set of activities is well defined (see Table 6.1), allowing us to **associate an estimated effort with the execution of each task.** For instance, we can estimate the workload required to deliver an advocacy project, an effort which, through standard project management practices, can be broken down into more specific, quantifiable activities.

The variables outlined in Table 6.3 can be linked to a numerical scale which, when applied to the effort associated with each activity cluster, yields an indicative estimate of the number of Full-Time Equivalents theoretically required to carry out the full scope of assigned responsibilities.

This theoretical model must then be **reconciled with a number of contextual factors,** such as resource availability, the strategic importance attributed to the PA function, and the organizational sizing methodologies adopted by each company.

The following Box 6.3 explores the importance of Coaching in PA as a tool for continuous improvement. An effective coach in this field must be aware of the distinctive features of Public Affairs Management in order to understand the innovative situations in which their role is carried out

---

Box 6.3 Coaching in Public Affairs

Definition and Purpose of Professional Coaching

Professional coaching is a structured, goal-oriented process that supports individuals in enhancing their self-awareness, behavioral effectiveness, and decision-making capacity in complex and dynamic environments. Unlike training – which primarily focuses on the transfer of knowledge and technical skills – coaching is designed to **unlock individual potential** through guided reflection, open dialogue, and personalized feedback.

In the context of PA, coaching plays a particularly valuable role. It helps professionals navigate institutional complexity, refine their ability to influence diverse stakeholders, and strengthen their leadership posture in politically sensitive environments. Rather than offering predefined answers or technical instructions, coaching encourages the professional to explore their own resources, test strategic approaches, and refine personal effectiveness in real time.

Why Coaching Is Particularly Relevant in Public Affairs

The unique nature of PA makes coaching not just useful, but often essential. The function operates at the intersection of external institutional expectations and internal strategic priorities, under conditions that are frequently unstable, ambiguous, and exposed to public scrutiny.

First, **relational complexity** is a defining trait of PA work. Professionals must engage with a wide range of actors, each with distinct priorities and communication styles. Building and maintaining trust across this heterogeneous stakeholder ecosystem requires not only technical know-how but also **emotional intelligence** and **political sensitivity**.

Second, the function involves a high degree of **personal exposure and visibility**. Especially at senior levels, PA professionals are directly involved in interactions with the company's top leadership, policymakers, and at times, the media. This requires a strong personal presence, the ability to **manage pressure**, and excellent judgment in navigating sensitive issues.

Third, PA operates within a **politically sensitive environment**, where decisions must often be made with limited information, under tight timelines, and with consequences that may impact the company's license to operate. In such settings, coaching offers a protected space to rehearse strategies, gain clarity, and develop adaptive leadership behaviors.

How Coaching Differs from Traditional Training

While both coaching and training are valuable tools for professional development, they differ significantly in approach, objectives, and impact.

Training is typically content-driven. It is delivered to groups, follows a structured agenda, and aims to build specific technical or methodological skills. The participant assumes the role of learner, receiving information and applying it within predefined parameters. Training is often time-bound and aligned with standardized learning outcomes, such as mastering policy analysis, understanding institutional frameworks, or using digital PA tools.

Coaching, by contrast, is a personalized process. It focuses on the individual's context, needs, and goals. Sessions are adaptive rather than fixed, and progress is measured by the professional's ability to act more effectively in their role, whether by strengthening influence, navigating institutional conflict, or managing personal visibility. The coachee is not a passive recipient but an active co-designer of the process, shaping each session through reflection and action.

In essence, training is about **learning new tools**, whereas coaching is about **using existing tools better**, with greater awareness, confidence, and alignment to strategic objectives. The two approaches are not in competition, but complementary: training builds competence; coaching builds presence, clarity, and influence.

How Coaching Differs from Mentorship

Although coaching and mentorship are often mentioned together, they serve distinct purposes and follow different dynamics. Mentorship typically involves a more experienced professional who **shares their knowledge**, offers advice, and provides guidance based on their own career path and personal lessons learned. It is often informal, relationship-driven, and centered on the mentor's experience as a model or reference.

Coaching, by contrast, does not rely on the transfer of personal experience or predefined solutions. Instead, it creates a structured, neutral space where the professional is encouraged to explore their own perspectives, test assumptions, and develop customized strategies. The coach does not provide answers but facilitates the coachee's discovery process, helping them unlock their potential and make choices aligned with their unique context and objectives.

6.3   Public Affairs Value Chain

The objective of this section is to identify **where value is generated** within PA activities and to provide a control tool for assessing **whether the function maintains a balanced effort** across its key tasks: gathering input, producing content, continuously sourcing relevant information, and transferring it externally.

To this end, we will divide the overall set of activities into **three macroprocesses**, examine their main characteristics, and highlight the key elements to be monitored in order to ensure they generate a tangible benefit for the company. In essence, we are adopting a different analytical lens compared to previous sections, one that is particularly useful for managing and steering the PA function.

We can break down the value chain of a PA function into three core components:

1. **Collection.** This phase focuses on gathering all relevant inputs that inform the PA agenda. It includes both structured and unstructured data, originating from institutional sources, stakeholder interactions, media monitoring, and internal business functions.
2. **Transformation.** In this phase, the collected inputs are analyzed, interpreted, and translated into strategic positions and engagement plans. It is the core moment where value is created through synthesis, judgment, and internal alignment.
3. **Transfer.** This final phase involves delivering the strategic output of the PA function to external stakeholders. It's the moment of execution, where influence is exercised, trust is built, and value is externalized.

6.3.1 Collection

An effective PA function gathers input in a balanced way from both internal and external sources, meaning from within the function itself, as well as from other corporate departments and external stakeholders. Internal input typically reflects operational planning based on the strategic objectives defined by the Chief. External input, on the other hand, may emerge at any time, either as urgent issues or as broader trends that require subsequent planning and alignment of activities.

Maintaining a **balanced mix of inputs is essential** for assessing the ongoing relevance of PA initiatives and ensuring their continued coherence with corporate objectives.

Figure 6.2 presents five different percentage distributions of *Internal/ Structured* versus *External/Reactive* collection. The optimal configuration is a 50/50 balance (*Strategic and Planned*), although values within a ±10% range are still considered excellent. The further the distribution deviates from this equilibrium, the more the function risks drifting toward a purely reactive role or, conversely, becoming insufficiently activated by other business units.

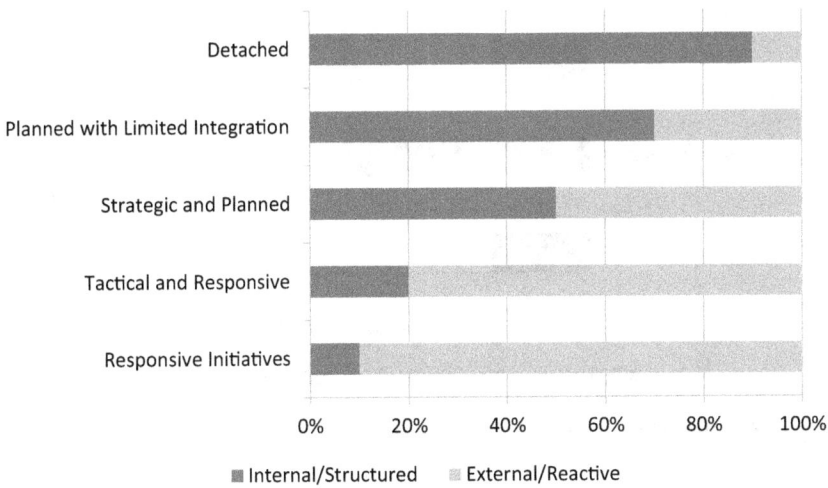

Figure 6.2 Internal and external collection.

6.3.2 Transformation

The *Transformation* phase is where real value is created. While the upstream and downstream stages allow for only limited creativity, often involving routine or standardized actions, this central phase offers a unique opportunity to enrich and adapt content in original, innovative, and impactful ways. Excelling at this stage requires robust tools for external benchmarking, as well as a critical focus on identifying and addressing any weaknesses in the proposition to ensure its effectiveness.

The Transformation phase can be further broken down into three stages: **Production, Elaboration,** and **Preparation.** More specifically:

- **Production** is the stage where all the raw content to be processed is assembled. To ensure a solid foundation, ideally at least 50% of the material should originate from the *Collection* phase, while the remainder should consist of content already available within the company or the PA function, along with additional input from external sources. These elements are essential for shaping the narrative and defining key messages. Figure 6.3 also illustrates cases where an overreliance on pre-existing content held by the PA function may lead to **self-referential positions** and a misalignment with actual priorities. Conversely, excessive use of external inputs may result in **positions that lack coherence and stability.** The percentage ranges presented should always be interpreted with a ±10% margin of tolerance.

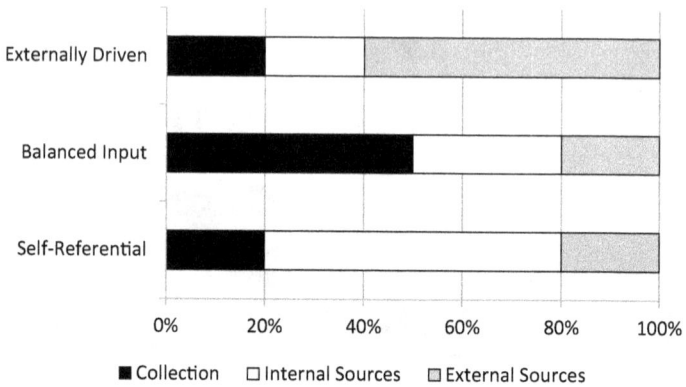

Figure 6.3 Transformation – Production phase.

- **Elaboration** is the core of the *Transformation* phase, where PA professionals refine content to enhance its strategic value. This process can vary in depth and is assessed through three key attributes:
  - *Competence*: evident in the consistency and quality of technical modifications to the input.
  - *Strategic Vision*: reflected in the integration of diverse sources into a cohesive message.
  - *Autonomy*: indicated by significant shifts in how the message is framed or structured, not just enriched, but reframed to suit strategic objectives.

The level of elaboration is classified as:

- **High,** when all three attributes are present.
- **Moderate,** when two are evident.
- **Low,** when only one is observed.

Low elaboration often results in technical support roles or superficial reworking. Moderate cases may show either vertical depth (expert content with limited integration) or horizontal breadth (good cross-functional synthesis without reframing). Only high-level elaboration delivers true strategic value through content that is technically sound, integrated, and autonomously repositioned.

- **Preparation** is the stage where elaborated content is tailored for subsequent **Transfer.** The nature of this activity varies significantly depending on whether the message is delivered directly to institutions or mediated through an intermediary. The framing of both positioning and messaging can shift considerably depending on the chosen channel. A well-balanced approach typically involves **70%** of the work focused on content intended for **direct transmission,** adapted to the selected channel, and **30%** dedicated to content to be conveyed **through intermediaries.**

Once the roles of **Production, Elaboration,** and **Preparation** have been clarified, it becomes essential to assess their relative weight in the process. This analysis not only illustrates how effort is distributed but also serves as a control tool, verifying whether the operational focus aligns with the intended organizational design.

The **optimal balance** is typically 30% *Production,* 40% *Elaboration,* and 30% *Preparation.*

6.3.3 Transfer

Let us now turn to the **Transfer** phase, the relational moment in which the company's positions are communicated externally. Here, we estimate the relative effort devoted by PA resources to three key areas:

- **Traditional Direct Engagement with institutions** (see Table 3.6).
- **Advocacy Activities** or, more broadly, relational efforts aimed at securing the active support of third parties.
- **DPA** initiatives (see Chapter 4).

Monitoring this final stage of the process offers a **clear indication of the strategic levers most frequently activated by the PA function.** As in other areas, there is no universally ideal distribution of effort. However, a balanced contemporary model might allocate approximately **50% to Traditional engagement, 40% to Advocacy,** and **10% to DPA** – with the understanding that DPA efforts embedded within broader advocacy projects are accounted for in the Advocacy category (see Section 3.5).

We now turn to a graphical representation of the effort distribution across the PA function. Taking the total activity as 100%, we can define ideal effort ranges for each of the three stages. In Figure 6.4, the areas corresponding to optimal values are shaded in light gray, while black bands highlight **suboptimal** percentages.

The **ideal trend** is shown as a dashed line. This curve reflects the effort required as we move closer to the institutional interface. Specifically, optimal intervals are defined as follows:

- **Collection:** 10% to 30%
- **Transformation:** 20% to 50%
- **Transfer:** 40% to 80%

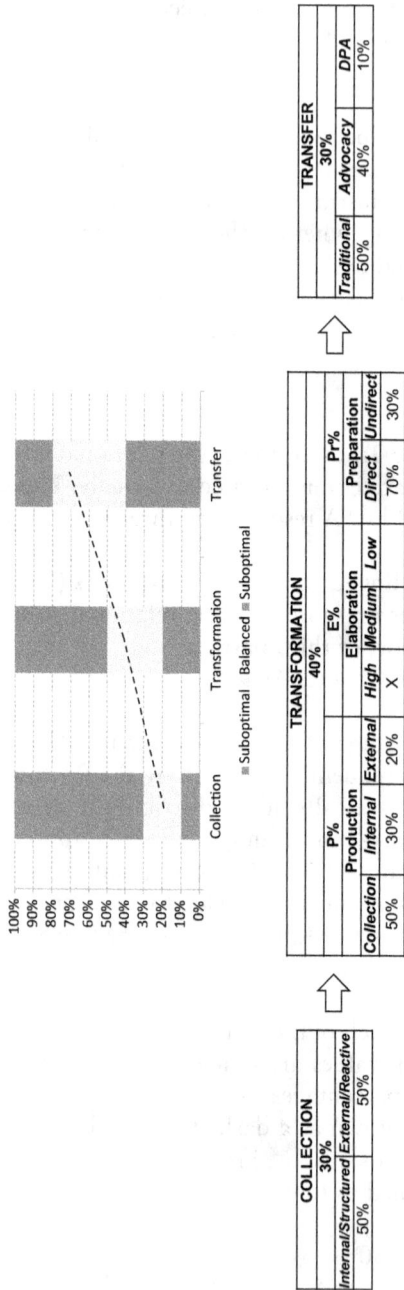

TRANSFER

30%		
Traditional	Advocacy	DPA
50%	40%	10%

TRANSFORMATION

P%		E%			Pr%	
Production		Elaboration			Preparation	
Collection	External	High	Medium	Low	Direct	Undirect
50%	20%	X			70%	30%

(Production: Collection 50%, Internal 30%, External 20%)

COLLECTION

30%	
Internal/Structured	External/Reactive
50%	50%

■ Suboptimal   Balanced ■ Suboptimal

Collection   Transformation   Transfer

Figure 6.4 Optimal effort allocation – Public affairs function.

6.4   Evaluating Public Affairs Performance

As with any other corporate function, the performance of PA must be assessed. Given its heterogeneous nature – as previously discussed – it is necessary to first distinguish between two broad categories based on the degree to which PA's contribution to an outcome can be determined:

1. **Clearly attributable PA contribution:** this occurs when the goal inherently involves institutional stakeholders and pertains exclusively to the company. This category is extensive and typically requires a significant effort by the PA function. Examples include: launching a public-private partnership, avoiding litigation, securing an incentive, or negotiating a regulatory exemption. In such cases, even if multiple corporate functions interact with the same public stakeholder, a well-structured internal system should **assign overall responsibility for managing the relationship** and achieving the institutional goal **to PA.** Consequently, the outcome, whether positive or negative, should be attributed to the PA function.
2. **Non-attributable or uncertain PA contribution:** this is the typical **case of lobbying.** When a legislative process concludes with the adoption of a regulation, it is clear that a broad range of actors contributed to the outcome: political parties, experts, businesses, associations, and others. This diversity is a guarantee of democratic pluralism. Our company's contribution is part of this mix, but – except in rare cases – it is impossible to isolate the specific impact of PA. In extreme scenarios, a favorable result may be achieved even without any lobbying effort.

In the first scenario, PA performance can be measured using standard corporate evaluation systems. The second is more complex. To address the ambiguity, a **dual evaluation** approach is often adopted, assessing two distinct aspects:

- **PA activities carried out to pursue the objective:** as discussed earlier, PA processes can be broken down into elementary tasks (see Tables 3.3 and 3.6), making it possible to measure tangible outputs such as number of meetings held, documents produced, or favorable media coverage. While these outputs do not directly confirm responsibility for the outcome, they provide a quantitative measure of the effort invested by PA personnel.
- **Level of objective achievement:** this involves assessing whether the goal was met, and if not, the extent to which it was partially achieved (if the goal is not binary/on-off in nature).

Combining these two dimensions enables the definition of a classic Management by Objectives target. However, it must be acknowledged that cases may arise in which positive activity assessments coexist with negative outcomes – or vice versa. In both instances, overall evaluations tend to be negative. The only truly rewarding case is one in which both the activities were appropriately executed and the intended outcome was achieved.

These traditional evaluation models can be further refined – or even progressively replaced – by **adopting a comprehensive PA performance framework**. However, they should still be retained for cases in which PA's contribution can be objectively verified. In the present volume, we have introduced a series of tools that allow for such linkages between PA actions and measurable outcomes. In Table 6.4, a set of tools is outlined that enables the explicit definition of PA objectives and corresponding evaluative actions. Four parameter classes are introduced: **Strategic, Relational, Operational, and Analytical**. By selecting one or more indicators from each category, appropriate combinations can be constructed to assess the various profiles within the PA function (see Section 6.1).

The table also highlights the **variables** that may be subject to evaluation, along with the **underlying rationale** for their inclusion. Furthermore, it is specified whether the parameter pertains to a **final outcome** or serves as an **intermediate checkpoint** during implementation. The final column identifies the PA profiles for which each parameter is most relevant.

6.5 Budgeting for Public Affairs Activities

The budget allocated to the PA function represents far more than a financial constraint: it is a **concrete indicator of the function's strategic recognition** within the organization. A well-funded PA department can operate with continuity, pursue medium- to long-term initiatives, and position itself as a proactive – rather than merely reactive – actor in navigating the institutional environment. In this sense, the budget becomes a key lever to assert the function's role and expand its external influence.

There is no such thing as a universally ideal budget for a PA function – neither in absolute nor relative terms – as numerous variables shape its definition. Factors such as the number of countries covered, the relevance and diversity of institutional stakeholders involved, and the company's lifecycle stage all significantly affect resource requirements. A localized unit with focused sectoral expertise will have very different financial needs compared to a global structure with a broader, cross-functional mandate. Accordingly, **budget allocation should be shaped around structural and strategic variables**, enabling a coherent and context-sensitive planning process.

Table 6.4 Outcome Measurement Variables for the Public Affairs Function

Variable	Reference	Possible Objectives	Rationale	Objective Type	PA Profile
Strategic Parameters					
Institutional Positioning Matrix	Figure 5.2	Improve the positioning of an institution within the matrix	Define strategies to seize opportunities, mitigate risks, or consolidate balance	Final	Chief, Institutional Relations Units, Advocacy and DPA Units
Corporate Strategic Relational Objectives	Figure 5.3	Improve the positioning and/or number of relevant stakeholders managed	Follow through on the defined corporate relational strategy	Final	Chief, Institutional Relations Units, Advocacy and DPA Units
Institutional Digital Positioning Matrix	Figure 5.4	Improve or maintain WSM parameters	Avoid risks or seize opportunities on digital/social channels	Final	Advocacy and DPA Units
Relational Parameters					
Value of the Personal Network	Table 2.7	Increase or maintain the current network value	Expand the relational network both qualitatively and quantitatively	Final	Chief, Institutional Relations Units
Value of Public Affairs Practices	Table 2.11	Increase or maintain the effectiveness of PA techniques	Ensure an effective Public Affairs function is in place	Final	All PA Units
Levels of Confidence in an Institutional Relationship	Table 3.7	Increase or maintain the level of trust with an identified institution	Strengthen the institutional relationship	Final	Chief, Institutional Relations Units

(Continued)

Table 6.4 (Continued)

Variable	Reference	Possible Objectives	Rationale	Objective Type	PA Profile
Relational Risk Profile	Figure 3.4	Reduce or maintain the Relational Risk Index	Reduce the impact of corporate issues on institutional relationships	Final	Institutional Relations Units
Operational Parameters					
Institutional Relationship Map	Figure 2.3	Generate consensus among selected stakeholders	Advance toward institutional goals by consolidating support	Intermediate	Institutional Relations Units, Advocacy and DPA Units
Objective Function and Result Indicator Function	Figure 2.7	Identify gaps between PA planning and actual developments	Verify alignment between PA plans and real-world developments	Intermediate	Institutional Relations Units, Advocacy and DPA Units
Public Affairs Technical Tools	Table 3.3	Achieve a positive result using a technical tool	Support relational needs through technical PA tools	Final or Intermediate	Institutional Relations Units, Chief PMO, Leadership Affairs Office
Actions of a Perfect Advocacy Project	Table 3.14	Implement a successful Advocacy project or initiative	Evaluate and track the execution of advocacy efforts	Final or Intermediate	Advocacy and DPA Units
WSM Action Plan	Table 4.4	Execute WSM activities in support of traditional ones	Use WSM tools effectively to enhance institutional engagement	Intermediate	Institutional Relations Units, Advocacy and DPA Units

Analytical Parameters

Institutional Stakeholder Profile	Figure 2.1	Develop and update institutional stakeholder profiles	Maintain an up-to-date overview of key institutions	Final	Institutional Relations Units, Chief PMO, Leadership Affairs Office
Web, Social and Media Relationship Map	Figure 2.4	Develop and update relationship maps for digital channels	Provide updated inputs for DPA-related planning and initiatives	Final	Advocacy and DPA Units, Chief PMO
Relational Risk Profile	Figure 3.4	Constant monitoring of relational risk	Ongoing monitoring of relational vulnerability	Final	Institutional Relations Units, Chief PMO, Leadership Affairs Office
Impact Map of Public Stakeholders	Figure 5.1	Map public stakeholders for strategic reporting purposes	Update strategic reporting with key institutional actors	Final	Institutional Relations Units, Chief PMO

Our focus here is not on the accounting exercise of estimating individual budget lines – a task that every company addresses through its own internal financial mechanisms – but rather on the **underlying logic** that drives the **formation of the PA budget**. Once this logic is clearly defined, the process of estimating and aggregating cost items becomes a more straightforward technical activity.

We begin, therefore, with the strategic mandate of the PA function. As outlined in Section 5.2, *the Institutional Corporate Strategy* may indicate three distinct trajectories for the strategic development of institutional relationships – each of which can be interpreted, from a budgeting perspective, as implying either an increase, a decrease, or a consolidation of resource allocation. Naturally, such guidance must be interpreted in light of the company's current relational positioning and the stage of its corporate lifecycle. This initial strategic signal – illustrated in Figure 5.3 – is especially important, as it allows us to immediately grasp the degree of strategic relevance assigned to PA within the organization.

To identify the relevant cost components, we refer to the *PA Management Model* (Figure 5.6), focusing exclusively on the **typical PA-related expenses** and excluding general overhead costs that derive from the company's broader organizational setup, such as IT systems, communication tools, office space, real estate, and security. The first column of Table 6.5 lists the

Table 6.5 Main Public Affairs Budget Items

Activity Layer	Typical Budget Items
Strategic Institutional Engagement	Organization and support of high-level meetings with institutional stakeholders Participation in political forums and policy roundtables (national or international) Executive travel and representation expenses Investments in high-profile institutional visibility initiatives
Strategic Definition and Alignment	Strategic consulting for scenario analysis and policy forecasting Executive workshops with top management on PA objectives and positioning Regulatory impact assessments and sectoral studies
Advocacy Implementation and Institutional Projects	Development and dissemination of position papers and institutional materials Management of advocacy campaigns Engagement of legal firms or specialized communication agencies Organization of thematic events (policy forums, institutional breakfasts)

(Continued)

Table 6.5 (Continued)

Activity Layer	Typical Budget Items
Institutional Relationship Management	Membership fees for associations and think tanks Sponsorships Travel and representation expenses
Integrated Digital Influence Activities	Production of institutional digital content (videos, infographics, articles) Management of digital advocacy campaigns on social platforms Costs for influencers Tools for mapping digital stakeholders, sentiment analysis on digital channels
Insight Generation, Intelligence Processing, and Content Development	Production of strategic analyses and internal briefing materials Predictive analytics software (AI) and issue-based tracking tools Management of periodic reports and customized alerts for top executives
Operational and Service Interactions	Logistical costs to support operational institutional requests
Institutional Monitoring and Data Repository	Subscriptions to legislative monitoring services Institutional databases and shared document repositories Maintenance and updating of the institutional knowledge base

model's *Activity Layers*, while the second column details the characteristic budget items associated with each layer.

Still referring to the model presented in Figure 5.6, some of the listed activities can be carried out internally, while others may be outsourced. For equivalent scopes of activity, internal development naturally requires a greater number of human resources, for which the key sizing variables have been outlined in Table 6.3.

Ensuring that the function has a budget aligned with its operational needs depends largely on the **negotiating capacity of the** *Chief Public Affairs Officer,* who plays a pivotal role in the budgeting process, from the initial proposal to ongoing monitoring and control. It is their responsibility to identify, in coordination with peer functions, opportunities for cost-sharing linked to shared goals or cross-functional initiatives.

Bibliography

Bolman L.G., Deal T.E., *Reframing Organizations: Artistry, Choice, and Leadership*, Jossey-Bass – Wiley, Hoboken (New Jersey), 2021.
Cockins G., *Performance Management: Integrating Strategy Execution, Methodologies, Risk, and Analytics*, Wiley, Hoboken (New Jersey), 2009.

Datar S., Rajan M., *Horngren's Cost Accounting: A Managerial Emphasis*, Pearson, London (UK), 2017.

Di Giacomo G., *Institutional Marketing & Public Affairs: Managing Institutional Relations to Create Value for the Business*, Franco Angeli Editore, Milan (IT), 2019.

Jones G., *Organizational Theory, Design, and Change*, Pearson, London (UK), 2012.

Musters R., Ellora J.P., Surya R., *Organizing the government affairs function for impact*, McKinsey Quarterly, 2013. https://www.mckinsey.com/capabilities/strategy-and-corporate-finance/our-insights/organizing-the-government-affairs-function-for-impact

Neely A., *Business Performance Measurement: Theory and Practice*, Cambridge University Press, Cambridge (UK), 2002.

Washington E., Griffiths B., *Competencies at Work: Providing a Common Language for Talent Management*, Business Expert Press, New York, 2015.

Wihtmore J., *Coaching for Performance, 6th edition: The Principles and Practice of Coaching and Leadership: Fully Revised Edition*, John Murray Business, London, 2024.

Index

For Product Safety Concerns and Information please contact our EU
representative GPSR@taylorandfrancis.com
Taylor & Francis Verlag GmbH, Kaufingerstraße 24, 80331 München, Germany